TEMPLES OF KṚṢṆA IN SOUTH INDIA

HISTORY, ART AND TRADITIONS IN TAMILNĀḌU

TEMPLES OF KṚṢṆA IN SOUTH INDIA

HISTORY, ART AND TRADITIONS IN TAMILNĀḌU

T. Padmaja

ABHINAV PUBLICATIONS

abhinav publications

First published in India **2002**

Publishers
Shakti Malik
Abhinav Publications
E-37 Hauz Khas
New Delhi-110016 (INDIA)
Phones: 6566387, 6562784, 6524658
Fax: 91-11-6857009
e-mail: shakti@nde.vsnl.net.in
Website: http://www.abhinavexports.com

ISBN 81-7017-398-1

Phototypesetting and Processing by
Onkar Digital Studio
C-50, Sharda Puri
Mansarovar Garden
New Delhi-110015

Printed at
D.K. Fine Art Press Pvt. Ltd.
Ashok Vihar, Delhi

CONTENTS

PREFACE

The present book embodies the results of my research work done in the Department of Ancient History and Archaeology, University of Mysore since 1983 under the guidance of Dr. A.V. Narasimha Murthy, Professor and Head. I owe a deep sense of gratitude to him for his constant encouragement and valuable guidance all through. I thank the authorities of the University of Mysore for the opportunity given to me to undertake this work and permitting me to publish the thesis.

I should also express my gratitude to the French Institute of Indology, Pondicherry, the American Institute of Indian Studies, Varanasi and the Archaeological Survey of India, Chennai Circle and Temple Survey Project, Chennai and the Director, Government Museum, Chennai, for supplying some of the photographs illustrated here. I also thank the Indian Council of Historical Research, New Delhi for their financial support. I thank Dr. Nanditha Krishna, Director of C.P. Ramaswami Aiyar Institute of Indological Research, Chennai for her keen interest in, and help and encouragement for this study.

My sincere thanks are due to several scholars who spared their valuable time for discussions with me and particularly to my father Prof. K.V. Raman, Chennai University, Padma Bhushan Shri K.R. Srinivasan, Prof. C. Jagannathachari and Dr. T. Vaithamanithy, my father-in-law. I also acknowledge my thanks to Prof. Raju Kalidass, Tamil University, Thanjavur, Shri V.K. Rajamani and Dr. Chitra Viji for kindly lending some of the photographs reproduced in this volume; my husband Shri V. Thiruvengadathan for his valuable support and Shri R. Venkatesan who helped in photo documentation of sculptures and bronzes. I also thank Shri Shakti Malik of Abhinav Publications, New Delhi for publishing this work.

Chennai **T. Padmaja**

ABBREVIATIONS

AHN	*Ahanānūru*
ARE	*Annual Report of Epigraphy*
BG	*Bhagavat Gītā*
BGP	*Bhāgavata Purāṇa*
HV	*Harivamsa*
JIH	*Journal of Indian History*
KLT	*Kalithokai*
MBH	*Mahābhārata*
MDK	*Maduraikānchi*
MTV	*Mudal Tiruvantāti*
NTM	*Nācchiyār Tirumoḻi*
NTV	*Nānmukan Tiruvantāti*
Perum	*Perumpānārruppaḍai*
Periya T.M.	*Periya Tirumaḍal*
Perumāl T.M.	*Perumāl Tirumoḻi*
PRN	*Puranānūru*
PRP	*Paripāḍal*
PTM	*Periyāḷvār Tirumoḻi*
RV	*Ṛg Vēda*
SII	*South Indian Inscriptions*
SLP	*Silappadikāram*
TAS	*Travancore Archaeological Series*
TCV	*Tiruchanda-viruttam*
TPV	*Tiruppāvai*
TVM	*Tiruvāymoḻi*
V.Bh.	*Villibhāratam*
VSMRS	*Vaiṣṇavism, Saivism, Minor Religious Systems* by Bhandarkar, R.G. (1913)

LIST OF ILLUSTRATIONS

22. Bakāsura-vadha, Varadarajaswami Temple, Kanchi.
23. Gōvardhanadhāri-Kṛṣṇa, Kanchi.
24. Navanīta-chora (Kṛṣṇa stealing butter), Tiruvendipuram.
25. Navanīta-chora, Varadaraja Temple, Kānchi.
26. Navanīta-chora, Tirukkunrungudi.
27. Kṛṣṇa and Balarāma stealing butter, Vrinjipuram.
28. Kṛṣṇa tied to the mortar, Kānchi.
29. Kṛṣṇa undergoing punishment, Vellore.
30. Navanīta Kṛṣṇa, Seramādēvi.
31. Navanīta Kṛṣṇa, Satyamangalam.
32. Navanīta-Nritta Kṛṣṇa, Madurai.
33. Navanīta-Nritta Kṛṣṇa, Tirupuvanam.
34. Navanīta-Nritta Kṛṣṇa, Pallikonda.
35. Navanīta-Nritta Kṛṣṇa, Pallikonda.
36. Nardhana Kṛṣṇa in Chatura-tandava, Uttarakosamangai.
37. Nardhana Kṛṣṇa.
38. Kṛṣṇa in Chatura-tandava, Nerūr.
39. Nardhana-Kṛṣṇa.
40. Nardhana-Kṛṣṇa.
41. Nardhana-Kṛṣṇa.
42. Nardhana-Kṛṣṇa (sculpture), Srinivasanallur.
43. Kāliyanardhana, Sriperumbudur.
44. Kāliyanardhana, National Museum, New Delhi.
45. Kāliyanardhana (Locality not known).
46. Kāliyanardhana, Tiruppullani.
47. Kāliyanardhana, Thanjavur.
48. Kāliyanardhana, Thanjavur Dt.
49. Nāga stone with Kṛṣṇa, Sevilimedu (near Kānchi).

INTRODUCTION

The origin of Kṛṣṇa worship is steeped in antiquity. Some would trace it back to the epic *Mahābhārata* and some would take it still earlier to the *Upanishads* and the *Vēdas*. But whatever is its antiquity, it cannot be denied that this ancient cult became a very popular and widespread one all over India cutting across the barriers of language, regions, sects and even races. Great philosophers and poets belonging to different parts of India were fascinated by the many-sided personality of Kṛṣṇa and have composed poems, epics, lullabies in their respective languages which have enriched the Kṛṣṇa lore. Over the centuries, Kṛṣṇa was not only a source of inspiration for the philosophers and religious leaders who gave their own interpretations of his teachings (contained in the *Bhagavat Gītā*) but also popular at the folk level as seen in the popular village festivals, street dramas, folk dances from Saurashtra to Assam and from Mathura and even Nepal to Kanyakumari. The spread of this cult to different parts of India and its impact on the local religion, literature, temples, sculptures and paintings would form an important field of research which is still largely unexplored. Though some valuable attempts have been made to study the origin and spread of the Kṛṣṇa cult in general, there is considerable scope for an intensive regional study, particularly of South India.

The present work undertakes such a study with regard to Tamilnāḍu. It traces the origin and development of Kṛṣṇa worship (or Bhāgavatism) in this southern extreme part of India. It focuses attention on the impact of Kṛṣṇa cult on the religion, temple and folk traditions, art and architecture particularly from about 7th to the end of the 17th century A.D., from the period of the Bhakti movement to the period of the Vijayanagar Nāyak rule in Tamilnāḍu.

Sources

Tamil, one of the oldest languages of India, has an ancient and rich body of literature. The earliest extant works commonly known as the Sangam Literature are datable at least to the early centuries of the Christian era. They are comparatively free from Sanskrit influence and so provide valuable data on the history of the spread of the northern religions, faiths, institutions and the like in the extreme south. They also furnish information on the interaction of the northern and southern traditions and their adaptations and synthesis.

The Sangam classics provide the background for the rise of Kṛṣṇaism in the Tamil country. The period of the Tamil Bhakti movement between sixth and ninth century A.D. produced devotional Tamil literature of the Āḷvār saints centring round Viṣṇu and His various forms and especially Kṛṣṇa, which is another valuable source material for this period. The four thousand Tamil hymns (*Nālāyara-Divyaprabandham*) show how the Tamil saints drew inspiration from Kṛṣṇa's personality, his life and teachings. A detailed analysis of this literature is presented here.

The post-Bhakti literature viz. the commentaries of the Vaiṣṇava āchāryas on the hymns of the Āḷvārs form another important source to trace the development of Kṛṣṇa worship in Tamilnāḍu. There were Tamil renderings of the epic *Mahābhārata* such as those of Perundevanar's (9th century A.D.) and Villiputtūrār's (15th century) which help us to know the growing popularity of the Kṛṣṇa worship. The *Sthalapurāṇas* of the Viṣṇu temples of Tamilnāḍu throw light on the myths and traditions that grew round the temples.

The numerous inscriptions found on the walls of the Viṣṇu temples of Tamilnāḍu and the copper plate grants of the Pallavas, the Pāṇḍyas and the Chōḷas and the Vijayanagar form another major source material. They throw light on the history and growth of the Kṛṣṇa temples in Tamilnāḍu at various times, the patronage extended to them by the kings, nobles, merchants, the shepherd class and indeed various sections of Tamil society. They also tell us about the festivals that were celebrated for Kṛṣṇa. Copper plate grants contain references to the great esteem in which Kṛṣṇa was held by the several royal dynasties of the Tamil country.

The beautiful sculptural panels on the Kṛṣṇa theme, the exquisite bronze images of Kṛṣṇa in various forms, the wood works and the paintings that abound in Tamilnāḍu show how the Kṛṣṇa theme permeated the art heritage of Tamilnāḍu and form a valuable source for this study. In fact, the Tamil sculptors, bronze makers, wood carvers, painters and ivory carvers have left us a rich legacy of art devoted to Kṛṣṇa theme which deserves a careful study and appreciation.

In Chapter I the origin of Kṛṣṇa worship is traced back to Sanskrit religious literature. The Sanskrit works like the *Ṛg Vēda*, the *Upanishads*, the epics and the *Purāṇas* give us valuable information about the antiquity of the cult and particularly the works like the *Harivamsa, Viṣṇupurāṇa* and the *Bhāgavata Purāṇa* throw welcome light on the development of Kṛṣṇa worship from a folk or pastoral cult to the absorption in the pan-Indian pantheon. The chapter then goes on to discuss the advent of Kṛṣṇa cult in Tamil religious tradition as revealed in the Tamil Sangam works, the oldest extant body

1. Ādinātha Perumāḷ Temple, Āḷvār Tirunagari, Main Vimana showing Kṛṣṇa sculptures.

2. Ādinātha Perumāḷ Temple, Nammāḷvār shrine, Kṛṣṇa sculptures in the *kūdu* arches.

3. Ādinātha Perumāḷ Temple, Āḷvār Tirunagari, Kṛṣṇa with Rukmini and Satyabhama (Window decoration in Nammāḷvār shrine).

84. Pārthasārathi, Triplicane, Madras.

85. Pārthasārathi, Triplicane, Madras.

92. Kṛṣṇa with butter pot, Thanjavur.

72. Rājamannār, Mannargudi.

103. Viṣṇu-chitta (Periyāḷvār), Srivilliputtūr.

104. Āṇḍāḷ with Rangamannār, Srivilliputtūr.

105. Nammāḷvār, Alwar Thirunagari.

of Tamil literature. This literature is quite rich in its references to different aspects of the personality of Kṛṣṇa and allusions to the episodes connected with his life. The Tamil epic *Silappadikāram* of a slightly later date (c. 5th century A.D.) presents a remarkable portrayal of Kṛṣṇa in association with the cowherds in whose company he performed dances of different types. Some of the peculiar aspects of Kṛṣṇa cult that developed along the indigenous lines of tradition are discussed.

The worship of Panchavīras and the association of Kṛṣṇa with Nappinnai (peculiar to Tamil tradition) are also dealt with in this chapter. Many interesting points such as the association of the Tamil kings of the Pāṇḍyan and Āy dynasties with the Pāṇḍavas of the *Mahābhārata* fame and the Yādava (cowherd clan) respectively are examined in the light of the Tamil literary and epigraphical data. The pastoral character of Kṛṣṇa appealed to the Tamils and they honoured him as the Lord of the *mullai* or forest region. In brief, this chapter forms the background for the early spread of Kṛṣṇa worship in Tamilnāḍu and the process of its absorption into the Tamil social and cultural milieu.

Chapter II analyses the place occupied by Kṛṣṇa cult in Tamil religion as reflected in the literature of the Bhakti movement which was in full swing between 600 to 850 A.D. This movement had both the Vaiṣṇava and Saiva streams. As the Kṛṣṇa cult is essentially Vaiṣṇava in its character, naturally the Vaiṣṇava religious works and temple festivals and rituals are to be carefully studied.

The great Tamil work *Nālāyira-Divya-Prabandham* a collection of 4000 hymns of the twelve Vaiṣṇava saints, called the Āḷvārs, is taken up for a detailed study. We take up the Āḷvārs' works one by one and see how the Kṛṣṇa theme became dominant in their hymns. We see in their hymns an intense emotional ecstasy for the *avatāras* of Viṣṇu especially Kṛṣṇa in his multifarious facets. Periyāḷvār assumed the role of the mother Yasōdā and sang lullaby and other hymns which constitute a special class of Tamil poetry called *piḷḷai-tamil.* He has described the mother's joy at every stage in the growth of the child. For his daughter Āndāl, Kṛṣṇa was her lover and lord and her poems are inspired by the *nāyaka-nāyaki-bhāva.* For Nammāḷvār Kṛṣṇa was his life-breath. He saw him "in his food, drinking water and even the betel leaves he munched." In the poems of the Āḷvārs, we see the example of bridal mysticism and frustration and anger during separation and joy in union, *viraha-bhakti,* i.e. the devotion of the lovelorn lady for her sweetheart. All the *purāṇic* episodes connected with Kṛṣṇa's life are extensively described by them. In fact, some of the episodes not found in the Sanskritic purāṇas are alluded to by them.

Chapter III deals with the Kṛṣṇa tradition in the two categories of literature that appeared in Tamilnāḍu in the post-Bhakti period i.e. after 850 A.D.: (1) Srī-Vaiṣṇava religious works and (2) other general Tamil works. Under the former category, the works of the Vaiṣṇava *āchāryas* like Nāthamuni, Yāmunāchārya, Rāmānuja, Piḷḷai Lōkāchārya, Vēdānta Dēsika and others are analysed. The well-known Vaiṣṇava preceptor Rāmānuja was a great devotee of Kṛṣṇa and wrote his commentary on the *Gītā*. He expounded his famous Visiṣṭādvaita philosophy based on the *bhakti* and *prapattimārga* (path of surrender) propounded by the Āḷvārs earlier. Several works in Tamil and Sanskrit appeared on the Kṛṣṇa theme, like Vēdānta Dēsika's *Yādavābhavudaya* and *Gōpalavimsati*.

Another important class of Srīvaiṣṇava literature is the commentaries (Vyākhyānas) on the Āḷvārs' hymns that appeared between 11th and 15th centuries. These were written in the *manipravāla* style, a combination of Tamil and Sanskrit. The commentaries of Nampiḷḷai, Periavāchān Piḷḷai, Piḷḷai Lokāchārya, Aḷagiya Manavāḷa Nayanār and Manavāla Mahāmuni are famous and they contain scintillating thoughts and comments on the Bhāgavatism Visiṣṭādvaita-Vedānta and Kṛṣṇa's glories. They reflect an important stage in the development of Srī Vaiṣṇava theology of the Rāmānuja school which had profound influence on many Bhakti schools of later periods.

The second category of literature is general in nature and includes Tamil renderings of the *Mahābhārata* and the *Bhagavat Gītā*. Here important works like Perundevanar's *Bhārata-venba*, Villiputturar's *Bhāratam*, Srī Baṭṭanār's work *Paramārtha Darsanam*, Piḷḷai Perumāḷ Ayyangar's works have been used. Jayankonḍār's *Kalingathuparani* and Oṭṭakuthar's *Mūvar-Ula* also contain interesting references to Kṛṣṇa theme and attest to the widespread popularity of the Kṛṣṇa worship.

Chapter IV identifies temples and shrines specially dedicated to Kṛṣṇa in different parts of Tamilnāḍu and trace their traditions and history. The *Sthalapurāṇas* and the present-day rituals and festivals of the temples have preserved the popular myths and traditions that have grown round the temples. Here, we focus attention on the localisation of myths which form an interesting process of popularising the Kṛṣṇa worship.

The numerous inscriptions found in the temples of Kṛṣṇa and Viṣṇu in general provide us with the authentic historical data on the temples, the patronage they received from the royal dynasties like the Pallavas, Pāṇḍyas, Chōḷas, Vijayanagar and other chieftains, nobles and even the common folks. The close involvement of the different sections of the Tamil society in fostering the care of the Kṛṣṇa temples is revealed in the inscriptions. Each generation took pride in adding some new facets to the temples by way of additional shrines, *maṇḍapas* or introducing new festivals and services. The data from nearly 50 temples is studied in their historical context.

Chapter V shows how Kṛṣṇa theme inspired the Tamil artists—the sculptors, the metal icon makers, the painters, the wood and ivory carvers through many centuries. We have many superb examples of Kṛṣṇa sculptures of the Pallava period at places like Māmallapuram, Kānchi and Tiruvellarai. In the Chōḷa period, we see the sculptors in stone and metal vying with one another in giving expression to complex themes and episodes. Tamilnāḍu has produced many masterpieces of bronze icons depicting Kṛṣṇa in various poses—Bālakṛṣṇa, Navanīta Kṛṣṇa, Kāliya Kṛṣṇa, Rājagōpāla, Santānagōpāla, Vēnugōpāla, Pārthasārathi, Gītāchārya etc.

There are hundreds of Kṛṣṇa images in stone and metal belonging to the Chōḷa, Pāṇḍya and Vijayanagar periods displaying a variety of themes and expressions coming from different parts of Tamilnāḍu. Certain new forms were introduced in metal icons in the Chōḷa and Vijayanagar periods. Such stylistic and thematic trends are discussed in their historical context.

There are rare paintings of the *Bhāgavata Purāṇa* and other Kṛṣṇa themes in the temples of Tamilnāḍu belonging to the 15th and 16th centuries. This was also the period when wooden chariots were made in large numbers. They carry exquisite wood carvings of Kṛṣṇa theme as seen at Srirangam, Kānchi, Srivilliputtur etc. We also have some specimens of ivory carvings of Kṛṣṇa theme in Srirangam temple. A detailed documentation of the above-mentioned art productions and critical study thereof is presented in this chapter which is illustrated with more than 100 photographs, many of them for the first time.

Chapter I

KṚṢṆA IN EARLY SANSKRIT AND TAMIL TRADITIONS

The origin and development of Kṛṣṇa cult is shrouded in antiquity and it embodies several strands and strata from diverse sources. Scholars who have traversed this ground of enquiry have realised the complexity of the problem. The sources are vast, the *Vēdas*, the *Upanishads*, the epic *Mahābhārata*, the *Purāṇas*, the non-Vēdic like the Jaina works and the non-Sanskritic sources, especially early Tamil literature, the folklore, the epigraphical sources and so on and out of them all emerges a personality at once human, charming, friendly, charismatic, heroic, philosophical and divine. Some scholars wonder whether he could have been a historical figure. Some like Bhandarkar would take him as a religious teacher like the Buddha or Mahāvīra. Some would circumvent the difficulty by propounding many Kṛṣṇas from different sources. But a majority of scholars, especially historians, are of the opinion that the life of Kṛṣṇa has arisen from some basic kernel of a historical person who was apotheosised in the course of centuries. As Hardy observes: "Thus it does not seem impossible that a 'purely human' personality of whom the *Mahābhārata* and the *Purāṇas* have preserved vague memories forms one of the historical cornerstones of Kṛṣṇa figure. But what is much more important is the fact that the belief in his historicity remained a productive element in the theology of Kṛṣṇa."[1]

Here we briefly outline the development of Kṛṣṇa worship in the early Sanskrit tradition as a background to analyse and understand how far the different aspects of this tradition had their impact on the early religious tradition of Tamilnāḍu.

Kṛṣṇa in Early Sanskrit Tradition

The earliest references to the name Kṛṣṇa appear in the *Ṛg Vēda.* He is mentioned as a renowned seer.[1a] There is also mention of a Kṛṣṇa as a demon opposed to Indra in a struggle.[2] The former reference is important because it is further elaborated in the *Upanishads.*[3]

'Kṛṣṇa-Dēvakiputra' appears in the *Chāndōgya Upanishad*[4] as a student of Ṛṣi Ghōra Angīrasa who worshipped a deity manifested in the form of the sun. According to Raychaudhuri,[5] the doctrines similar to what Kṛṣṇa learnt from Ghōra were what he also taught in the *Bhagavat Gītā.* Here, one must note that Kṛṣṇa-Dēvakiputra was not known as 'Vāsudēva'; instead the name Acchutā, which appears as an epithet of Kṛṣṇa in the *MBH,* occurs in this work. The *Chāndōgya Upanishad,* a pre-Buddhist work, does not mention Vāsudēva—meaning son of Vasudeva—along with Dēvakiputra probably because the patronymic and matronymic of a person were not generally used together. The *Angīrasa* family to which Ghōra belonged was related to the Bhōjas,[6] who were like the Vṛṣṇis a sect of the *Yādava* clan.

On the basis of the commentaries on the *Aṣṭādhyāyi* and the Buddha *Ghaṭa Jātaka,* Prof. R.G. Bhandarkar forms his opinion[7] that the Brahmanical *gōtra* called *Kṛṣṇāyaṇa* sprang from an ancient sage named Kṛṣṇa with whom Vāsudēva of the *Kṛṣṇāyaṇa gotra* was identified at a later date. But, as D.C. Sircar says,[8] later traditions which state that a son of Vasudeva was called Kṛṣṇa owing to the colour of his complexion sound more reasonable. *Ghaṭa Jātaka* describes Vāsudēva as a scion of the royal family of upper Mathura. The deification of Kṛṣṇa took place quite early, perhaps in his lifetime.[9]

Patanjali (2nd century B.C.)[10] in his comment on *Pāṇini Sūtra* IV.3.98 states that the word Vāsudēva in the *sūtra* is the name of the one who is preeminently worshipful. Even during the time of Pāṇini, the names Vāsudēva and Kṛṣṇa were synonyms. It is clear from the *Pāṇini Sūtra* III.1.26 which mentions the vanquished as the Kamsa-pakṣa and the victorious as Vāsudēva-pakṣa. *Sūtra* VI.3.6 says "Janardana with himself as fourth", that is Kṛṣṇa with three other companions.[11] The three were Samkarṣaṇa, Pradyumna and Aniruddha. So, the worship of Vāsudēva-Kṛṣṇa must have been quite popular even in the time of Pāṇini whose date has been fixed about 400 B.C.[12]

The worship of Vāsudēva-Kṛṣṇa was also known as the Bhāgavata or the Panchavīra cult in the early days. According to the epics and the *Purāṇas,* the ruling clan of Mathura was called *yadu,* which was divided into various sects. The Vṛṣṇi sect to which Vāsudeva-Kṛṣṇa belonged was popular in later Vēdic times as we have plenty of references to it in the *Samhitās* and the *Brāhmaṇas.*[13] The heroes of the famous Vṛṣṇi clan, namely, Kṛṣṇa and Samkarṣaṇa were worshipped as gods as early as the time of Pāṇini.[14]

The earliest epigraphic evidence to the *Bhāgavata* religion is found in the 2nd century B.C.[15] The Besnagar inscription of Heliodorus dated 1st century B.C. is a significant one from which we know that even some Greeks became the followers of the *Bhāgavata* cult. Recent excavations in Besnagar by Khare reveal the fact that there might have been temples for the other four Vṛṣṇi heroes also. Evidences of other flag-staffs (*dhvajas*) for the heroes like the Garudadhvaja have come to light in the excavations. Some coins of Agathocles of 2nd century B.C. found in Al-Khanoum, Bactria, contain the representation of Kṛṣṇa and Balarāma. The diadem wearing Kṛṣṇa on the coin is carrying a disk in one hand and conch in another and Balarāma is seen holding a mace and a plough. Brahmi and Greek letters are engraved on the coins. The most important epigraphical evidence is the well-known inscription at Mora which stands as a testimony for the wide popularity of the *Panchavīra* cult as early as 1st century B.C. The names of the five Vṛṣṇi heroes whose images are known to have been installed and worshipped in a temple are Samkarṣaṇa or Balarāma, Vāsudēva (sons of Vasudēva), Pradyumna, Samba (sons of Vāsudēva Kṛṣṇa) and Aniruddha (grandson of Vasudeva). In the Ghosundi (Rajasthan) inscription of the 1st century B.C. both Samkarṣaṇa and Vāsudēva are called *Bhāgavata* as well as *anihata* (unconquered) and *Sarvēswara* (supreme lord).[16]

The *Bhāgavata* religion centring around the Vṛṣṇi heroes originated with the Yādava-Sātvata-Vṛṣṇi people of Mathura region and probably with the migration of the Yādava tribes, spread to other regions, the Gujarat and Deccan. From Deccan, the cult of Vāsudēva-Kṛṣṇa spread to South India. The Chinna (Kṛṣṇa District, Andhra) inscription of Yajna-Sātakarni dated last quarter of 2nd century begins with an invocatory verse to Vāsudēva and indicates the progress of *Bhāgavatism* in the south.

The evolution of the Bhāgavata cult from its origin and its integration with the Brahmanical mainstream was a slow process, the outlines of which are visible here and there. In the *Mahābhārata,* Vāsudēva-Kṛṣṇa is glorified as a Vṛṣṇi hero several times.[17] Both Kṛṣṇa and Balarāma are mentioned as Vṛṣṇi-Vīras in the epic.[18] But the divinity of Kṛṣṇa-Vāsudēva is frequently questioned in the *MBH,* as we see Sisupāla questioning him all the time. But attempts have been made through some powerful characters in the epic to emphasise the supremacy of Kṛṣṇa-Vāsudēva. For instance, Bhīṣma calls Vāsudēva 'the eternal god mysterious, beneficent, and loving', whom the Brāhmaṇas, Kṣatriyas, Vaisyas and Sūdras worship by their devoted actions.[19] The doctrine of *avatāras* helped to a great extent the spread of Kṛṣṇa cult. In the *MBH* Kṛṣṇa is often praised as Viṣṇu, the supreme lord. In the *Bhīṣmaparvam,* the supreme spirit is addressed as Nārāyaṇa and Viṣṇu is identified with Vāsudēva.

The concept of *avatāras* seems to have developed in the epic period. Both Vāsudēva-Kṛṣṇa and Rāma were identified with Viṣṇu. The identification of Kṛṣṇa as an *avatāra* of Viṣṇu could have happened in two ways:

1) In order to establish the Bhāgavata religion the followers of Kṛṣṇa-Vāsudēva identified their God with Viṣṇu who had become the supreme deity in later Vēdic religion.

2) It could have been the other way. Seeing the popularity of the Kṛṣṇa-

Vāsudēva cult, *Viṣṇuism* embraced the Vṛṣṇi hero Kṛṣṇa into its fold as an *avatāra* of the supreme lord, just as it did with Rāma.

Most probably, the combination of the above two views would be the correct one. Kṛṣṇa-Vāsudēva cult must have felt secure to have become a part of the popular *Viṣṇuism.* The Vēdic *Viṣṇuism,* by embracing a pastoral religion into its fold, began to appeal even more to the ordinary people. Some scholars see the *Bhāgavatism* as a sort of a protestant movement against the Vēdic religion, but definitely not as strong as Buddhism or Jainism. It was a milder form of reformist movement. Though it regarded the Vēdic rituals and sacrifices as of minor importance and condemned the slaughter of animals, the new theistic religion centred around the idea of a supreme God (Hari or Viṣṇu) and emphasised the importance of devotion to him. In its ultimate form, as developed in the *Bhagavat Gītā, Bhāgavatism* merged with the mainstream of *Viṣṇuism.*

Now, the next logical question that arises is: why did Kṛṣṇa come to be identified with Viṣṇu and not with any other God? There are several reasons for this. The first and the foremost is both are said to be of solar race. Viṣṇu in the *RV* was a solar deity, though a minor one. Kṛṣṇa of the *Chāndōgya Upanishad* was a pupil of Ghōra Angirasa who was a worshipper of Āditya-Viṣṇu.

Secondly, Viṣṇu was associated right from the Vēdic times with the work of deliverance of mankind in distress. He is depicted as a great benefactor of mankind.[20] He is a preserver of *Dharma.*[21] These qualities of Viṣṇu qualify him to take incarnations to protect the people. Naturally, Kṛṣṇa, the great hero of the Vṛṣṇis and the centre of the theistic movement, was identified with Viṣṇu. We have definite historical evidence of Kṛṣṇa's association with Viṣṇu, the supreme God in the Besnagar inscription of 180 B.C.[22] which records the erection of *Garuda* column—a bird associated with Viṣṇu originally—to Vāsudēva. In the *MBH,* the supreme spirit is addressed as Nārāyaṇa and Viṣṇu and is identified with Vāsudēva. The *avatāra* concept is seen fully developed in the *Bhagavat Gītā.* Kṛṣṇa is identified as the supreme power who took birth in this world in every *yuga* to vanquish the evil and establish the Dharma (righteousness).[23] The *visvarūpa* form of Kṛṣṇa and the *vibhūti-yōga* in the *Bhagavat Gītā* are significant in the sense that Kṛṣṇa is considered as a "*pūrṇa avatāra*" while all the other *avatāras* are regarded as "*amsa avatāra*". This point will be elucidated further in a later context.

Regarding Viṣṇu-Nārāyaṇa-Kṛṣṇa relationship, Benjamin Preciado-Solis points out that very important traits later associated with Kṛṣṇa are conspicuously present in the *Vēdas* like the expansive character of Viṣṇu from a young boy or dwarf with a giant body (*RV* 1.155.6) or Puruṣa that grows from out of the Golden Germ (*Hiraṇyagarbha*). The *MBH* describes Nārāyaṇa as one whose dwelling is in the waters and puts these words in the mouth of a baby floating on a banyan tree in the infinite ocean: "The child Nārāyaṇa holds the entire world just as Puruṣa does and as the baby Kṛṣṇa does" (Yasodā saw the entire universe in the mouth of Kṛṣṇa).[23a]

The next major development in the Kṛṣṇa cult or Viṣṇuism is Kṛṣṇa as a pastoral God. The stories of Kṛṣṇa as a cowherd and his childhood pranks in Gōkula, the cowherd settlement, add a delightful touch to the character of Kṛṣṇa. They also make him the most popular deity throughout India. R.G. Bhandarkar is of the opinion that stories of Kṛṣṇa as a herdsman must have sprung from the Abhiras, tribal people who occupied the land between Madhuvana near Mathura to Anūpa and Ānarta, the regions about Dwārakā,[24] and they must have worshipped a cowherd deity whom they identified with Vāsudēva-Kṛṣṇa. The Yamunā region, the scene of Kṛṣṇa's childhood, was well known for its cattle even in the *Ṛg Vēdic* period.[25]

Kṛṣṇa's association with the cows is also probably derived from Viṣṇu's connection with the cow. Viṣṇu, in the *Ṛg Vēda,* is called "Gopa", meaning "protector of cows" or "herdsman".[26] Another *RV* verse describes the highest place of Viṣṇu as a dwelling of "many-horned, swiftly moving cows".[27] The *Boudhāyana Dharmasūtra* calls him 'Gōvinda' and 'Dāmōdara'—one with a cord round one's belly—i.e. herdsman. This idea was expanded in later works. Viṣṇu represents a fertility God and a vegetation God as explained by Gonda.[28] The pastoral character which was attributed to Kṛṣṇa was the result of the assimilation of Kṛṣṇa cult and Viṣṇuism.

The *Viṣṇu Purāṇa* and the *Harivamsa* give a detailed account of the episodes of Kṛṣṇa's boyhood. The childhood tales of Kṛṣṇa are of Purāṇic origin and thus they belong to the post-epic period. The *Harivamsa* was regarded as a part of the *MBH.* The *Purāṇas* which relate the Kṛṣṇa story were codified in the 3rd or 4th century A.D. The *Viṣṇu Purāṇa* describes the birth of man-God as a black Kṛṣṇa and his childhood pranks in Gōkula. The *Purāṇas* took some themes from the earlier works like the *Vēdas.* For instance, the conflict between Kṛṣṇa and Indra is reflected in later works by Govardhanagiri episode—Purāṇic version of an earlier allusion found in the *RV* with modification. Probably, the *HV* was the first to give the details of Kṛṣṇa's birth and early life in a cowherd community at Vraja.[29]

Schulberg has pointed out that "as Kṛṣṇa's triumphs multiplied and his cult spread throughout India, it generally superseded the worship of many other older deities. The conflict between the new cult and the old ones was reflected in symbolic tales of Kṛṣṇa's struggles with these ancient divinities."[30] The following episodes of Kṛṣṇa's early childhood support the above view. The Govardhanagiri episode describes the struggle between the Indra and the Kṛṣṇa cults and also the triumph of the latter over the former. The

Kāliyamardana episode explains how the Nāga cult was superseded by the Kṛṣṇa cult. This theory of the popularity of the Nāga worship in the Mathura region has received support in archaeological and sculptural works. Recent archaeological excavations conducted in the Mathura region have brought to light evidence attesting to the popularity of Nāga worship in two regions. Many Nāga temples have been discovered recently.

Another important development in the Kṛṣṇa worship took place during the period of *bhakti* literature in which the friendship of Kṛṣṇa with the *gōpikas* or the cowherd girls is highlighted. The main idea was to stress the significance of *bhakti* and surrender to God and the humbleness of Kṛṣṇa who was the darling of the cowherd community. But later works, like the *Bhāgavata Purāṇa,* started depicting Kṛṣṇa as a lover of Gopis extolling his childhood plays with the girls of Gōkula and introduced an element of excessive love (*prēma*) into his character. This new aspect attributed to Kṛṣṇa might have been due to his identification with Viṣṇu, noted for his compassion for all and particularly as a promoter of conception and protector of embryos referred to in the *Ṛg Vēda.*[31] All these qualities were attributed to Kṛṣṇa, as an incarnation of Viṣṇu, and his friendship with young cowherd girls when he was below twelve years old can be viewed in this context. This was magnified by the introduction of Rādhikā or Rādhā, whose name first appears in the *Brahma Vaivarta Purāṇa,* a late work and, of whom the early authentic works like *MBH, HV, VP* and *BG* are silent. Rādhā is however mentioned in the Prakrit work "Gāthāsaptasati", attributed to Hala the Sātavāhana king of 1st century A.D.[32] But Rādhā became popular from the 12th century A.D. The Rādhā-Kṛṣṇa cult appears as a philosophical system in the teachings of Nimbarka, who belonged to the 12th century A.D.[33] Jayadeva, who lived in the 13th century, wrote *Gīta-Gōvind* which deals with joyful union and pangs of separation of Rādhā and Kṛṣṇa.

All these various stories and themes added new colour and flavour to the cult and Kṛṣṇa became a complex figure with roots going deep into diverse sources like the *Ṛg Vēda,* the *Upanishads,* the Epics, the *Purāṇas* and the folk tradition. The Kṛṣṇa cult had become one of the dominant features of religious movment of India by the time of the Gupta age. The Gupta period witnessed a well-developed Kṛṣṇa-Vāsudēva cult. We get plenty of evidence for this in the form of temples, sculptures, literature, inscriptions and seals. The Imperial Guptas were devout *Bhāgavatas,* and the Gupta kings Chandragupta II, Kumāragupta and Skandagupta called themselves as "*Parama Bhāgavatas*" on their coins. Their dates approximately range from 300 to 460 A.D. Bhita seal No. 21 contains a legend in northern Gupta characters (*namo-bhagavate Vāsudēvaya*).[34] According to Marshall, this seal shows that Bhita possessed a temple of Vāsudēva in the Gupta period. The Dasāvatāra temple of Deogarh stands as a testimony to the well-developed Vaiṣṇava cult. The myths of Kṛṣṇa's life were also depicted in sculptures even before the Gupta period. We have Kṛṣṇa's Gōpikāvilāsa sculptures in Pahadpur. A series of Kṛṣṇāyaṇa stories appear in two door-jambs found at Mandor of 4th century A.D. R.C. Mazumdar has pointed out that in the inscriptions of the Gupta age there are references to temples or flag-staffs of the god Viṣṇu-Nārāyaṇa-Vāsudēva. He has also cited instances to show the spread of Bhāgavata cult throughout the length and breadth of India—Nepal and the upper regions of the Beas in the north, in Bengal in the east, in Kathiawar in the west. In South India some of the early Sātavāhana, Pallava, Pāṇḍya, Ganga and Chālukya rulers were devout Bhāgavatas.[35]

Kṛṣṇa in the Sangam Literature

In Tamilnāḍu we have a rich body of Tamil literature generally known as the Sangam literature attributable mostly to the first two or three centuries A.D. It reflects both the indigenous religious customs and practices and also the religious cults that came from the north. According to Prof. Nilakanta Sastri the literature reflects a composite culture and pan-Indian deities like Indra, Viṣṇu, Rāma, Kṛṣṇa, Siva, Muruga and Durgā were well known and honoured.

This vast body of literature consists of two major anthologies *Eṭṭuthokai* and *Pattupāṭṭu* (The Ten Idyls) besides the Eighteen Minor Poems called *Padineṉ-kīlkaṇakku.* The Tamil grammar work *Tolkāppiyam* is considered by the Tamil scholars as the earliest of the Tamil works available today. Some would put it earlier than the Sangam works. Some would, however, date it in the 1st century B.C.-A.D. in the light of the recent researches in the newly discovered Tamil-Brahmi inscriptions in Tamilnāḍu. The two epics *Silappadikāram* and the *Manimēkalai* are generally considered to be post-Sangam works datable to 5th or 6th century A.D. These three categories of works mentioned above contain valuable data on the social and religious history of Tamilnāḍu and hence they deserve a close examination.

The *Tolkāppiyam* speaks of various gods and associates each one with a particular geographical division of the Tamil country. There were altogether five such landscapes (*tiṇais*) among which *mullai* was one. Māyōn was the deity of the *mullai* or forest region. Māyōn means one who is black in colour equivalent of Kṛṣṇa in Sanskrit. One of the *Eṭṭuthokai* works refers to Viṣṇu as "*Māyōn anna māl varuikkāva an*".[37] Another Sangam work *Madurai Kānchi* refers to Viṣṇu and his birth-star (*ōnam*) as "*Māyōn-mēya-ōṇa-nan-nāl*".[38] The above two references are given to establish the fact that Māyōn was none other than Kṛṣṇa/Viṣṇu. There are numerous references to this fact in almost all the Sangam works. Apart from the epithet Māyōn, Viṣṇu has also been referred to as *Māyavan, Māmiyōn, Netiyōn, Māl* etc. in the Sangam collections. These names often appear in the early Tamil works to denote Kṛṣṇa too. *Kalithokai,*[39] one of the eight anthologies, refers to the episode of Kṛṣṇa killing the wrestlers sent by Kamsa as "*mallarai maramchaittha māl*".

Here, the epithet *Māl* is used for Kṛṣṇa. *Māyavan* is another epithet used frequently both for Viṣṇu and Kṛṣṇa.[40] *Māyavan* has also been translated as the "Great Dissembler". No wonder Kṛṣṇa is called *Māyavan* as he is well known for his mysterious activities. The usage of common names for both Viṣṇu and Kṛṣṇa in the Sangam works tends to show that the identification of Kṛṣṇa with Viṣṇu was an established fact during that period. Kṛṣṇa worship should have reached Tamil country only after the identification of Vēdic God Viṣṇu, Cosmic God Nārāyaṇa with the Vṛṣṇi hero God Vāsudēva-Kṛṣṇa had taken place in North India. As far as Tamiḻagam is concerned, Kṛṣṇa worship came along with Viṣṇu worship. The cult of Kṛṣṇa was apparently popular in ancient Tamiḻagam around the date of the *Tolkāppiyam.* If Kṛṣṇa was the chief deity of one of the divisions of land called *mullai,* then the Kṛṣṇa worship must have reached Tamil country a few centuries earlier. The pastoral nature of Kṛṣṇa seems to have had a great appeal for the Tamils. Especially, the people of the *mullai* region accepted him as their favourite God as he was born in their community. M. Raghava Iyengar is of the opinion that the God Māyōn referred to in the *Tolkāppiyam* was Kṛṣṇa himself, an *avatāra* of Viṣṇu.[42]

Māyōn, Māyavan, Māyan and Māl—all these names were the ancient Tamil names for both Kṛṣṇa and Viṣṇu. Māyōn, which denotes his black complexion, is an equivalent of Kṛṣṇa in Sanskrit. Wherever Kṛṣṇa and his childhood plays are mentioned in the Sangam collection, he is always referred to by these names.

Kaṇṇan

The epithet Kaṇṇan which was favourite name of Kṛṣṇa in Tamil literature of the Bhakti and later periods does not seem to have been used in the same connotation in the Sangam collection. A verse in the *Paripāḍal* describes Kṛṣṇa as the lotus-eyed (*tāmarai Kaṇṇan*).[43] But the word Kaṇṇan is always used with an adjective or a prefix. There were many poets known as Urittiran-Kannanār,[44] Kāri-Kannanār, Kumattūr Kannanār, Marutan Kannanār etc. Thus Kaṇṇan seems to have been a generic name, not specifically used for Kṛṣṇa. On the other hand we have names like Dāmōdaranār and Gōvardhanār exclusively to denote Kṛṣṇa.

The term Kaṇṇan denoting Kṛṣṇa was probably derived from the Prakrit word Khanna which according to the Buddhist *Ghaṭa Jātaka* is a *Gōtra* name. In the *Mahaummagga Jātaka,* Vāsudēva is mentioned as belonging to the Kaṇhāyana-gōtra. The name Khanna is even today widely prevalent in North

India. In Telugu, it is Kannaiya. The Tamil adoption and rendering of the Prakrit *Kanha* or *Khanna* would be Kaṇṇan which became popular in Tamil country in the *Bhakti* period. In the hymns of the *Āḻvārs*, and later works we see this name Kaṇṇan being extensively and exclusively used as an endearing term for Kṛṣṇa.

We will now analyse the various aspects of Kṛṣṇa lore found in the Sangam classics. The *Eṭṭuthokai* and *Pattupāṭṭu* collections contain a number of references to Kṛṣṇa and his brother Balarāma. During the Sangam period, people considered Kṛṣṇa as an incarnation of Viṣṇu and works like the *Ahanānūru* (verse 59) and the slightly later work *Paripāḍal* (verse 2) bear testimony to this fact.[45] The *Paripāḍal* speaks about the Panchavīra cult and the *avatāra* concept. It says "It is difficult even for the learned ascetics to predict the coming down of the God Tirumāl."[46] The 15th verse in the *Paripāḍal* presents Tirumāl as the very personification of love for his subjects and his other manifestations, Samkarṣaṇa and Vāsudēva as of great glory.[47] This shows clearly that *vyūha* concept was also known to the author of the *Paripāḍal.*

The *Puranānūru* verses refer to Kṛṣṇa along with Balarāma. In verse 56 the Pāṇḍya king Ilavandikaipaḷḷi-thunjiya Nanmāran is compared to Balarāma and Kṛṣṇa.[48] Their association with the palmyra and Garuda flags respectively is also mentioned. The *Puranānūru* refers to Kṛṣṇa and Balarāma along with Siva and Muruga as the four main deities.[49] It also describes Balarāma and Kṛṣṇa as the two great gods.[50] In this particular verse, the Chōḻa and the Pāṇḍya kings are compared to Balarāma and Kṛṣṇa. Kṛṣṇa's childhood sports and the *MBH* stories were all fairly popular during the Sangam period. In the *Puranānūru*[51] P.T.S. Iyengar sees a reference to the *Gītā* in the line "*Urai sāl sirappin pugaḷ sāl māra*". If the interpretation is correct, we have here perhaps the earliest reference to the *Gītā* as expounded by Kṛṣṇa. Another reference to the *Gitā* is also suggested in the *Maduraikānji.*[51a]

We get a number of references to Kṛṣṇa-*līlās* in the *Eṭṭuthokai* collection. The *Vastrāpaharaṇa* episode (Kṛṣṇa stealing the clothes of the cowherd girls) has been described in the *Ahanānūru.*[52] A *Kalithokai* verse[53] refers to Kṛṣṇa blowing the conch and Baladēva wearing only one earring. The epithet "*Oru Kulaiavan*" for Baladēva also occurs in the *Kalithokai* verse (26:1). The act of Kṛṣṇa killing the demon Kesi who came in the form of a horse is described in the *Kalithokai,*[54] and also the *Paripāḍal.*[55] The victory of Kṛṣṇa over the wrestlers is referred to in the *Kalithokai* more than once.[56]

Kalithokai also mentions a number of episodes from the *MBH.* The Bhārata war is described as a war between the 'Hundred' (*Nūrruvar*) and the 'Five' (*Aivar*) i.e. the hundred brothers of Kauvaras and the five brothers of Pāṇḍavas.[57] The bull fight arena (*toluvu*) is likened to the battleground of Kurukshētra.

The anthology of ten songs (*Pattupāṭṭu*) another major collection of Sangam poems has numerous references to Kṛṣṇa and his life episodes. One of them *Perumpāṇāṟṟupaḍai* describes Kṛṣṇa as Munnīr-vaṇṇan which means 'the blue coloured',[58] thus equating Kṛṣṇa with Viṣṇu. It also mentions that the ruler of Kānchi city, Iḷam Tiraiyan, as a descendant of Viṣṇu. In valour, he is compared to the Pāṇḍavas who vanquished their hundred enemies.[59] The *Maduraikānchi* assigns *ōnam* the birth-star of Viṣṇu to Kṛṣṇa clearly indicating that the Sangam people equated Kṛṣṇa with Viṣṇu.[60]

Post-Sangam Works

Silappadikāram

The two Tamil epics *Silappadikāram* and *Maṇimēkalai* which are taken by scholars as belonging to the post-Sangam period (5th or 6th century A.D.) give detailed accounts of a well-developed Kṛṣṇa cult. There are a number of references to Kṛṣṇa and his childhood feats in the *Silappadikāram*. By that time episodes of Kṛṣṇa's life, his consorts, and his divine qualities all became quite popular. References to *bālakrīḍās* of Kṛṣṇa like killing of the demons, dancing with the gopis, are found in plenty.

The section on the *Āycchiyar-Kuravai* (The Dance of the Cowgirls) in the *Silappadikāram* refers to the following feats of Kṛṣṇa as a child and then as a youth:

Child Kṛṣṇa stealing butter.[61]

Kṛṣṇa throwing a calf as a stick for plucking the woodapple.[62]

Kṛṣṇa killing the demon who appeared in the form of a *Kurunda* tree in the backyard of the house.[63]

Kṛṣṇa concealing the clothes of Nappinnai.[64]

Yasōdā, Kṛṣṇa's mother, tying his hands with a churning rope.[65]

Kṛṣṇa hiding the sun with the Chakra.[66]

Kṛṣṇa as a messenger of the Pāṇḍavas to the Kauravas.[67]

Kṛṣṇa destroying Kamsa's evil designs.[68]

These frequent references to Kṛṣṇa's acts of valour and childhood plays show that the *Harivamsa, Viṣṇu Purāṇa*, and the *Mahābhārata* stories were all very well known to the Tamils. Kṛṣṇa had been already accepted as their chief by the Āyars just as the Āhirs of North India as is clear from the "*Āycchiyar-Kuravai*" chapter. The Āyars considered their king as a form of Viṣṇu or Kṛṣṇa. *Silappadikāram* praises the Pāṇḍya king "whose chest was adorned with sandal paste obtained from Podigai hill, pearls obtained from the ocean and the *hāra* (necklace) presented by Indra, the God of the Dēvas, was none other than Kṛṣṇa who grazed the cattle of Gokula and destroyed the *Kurunda* tree."[69] The episode of "*Vastrāpaharaṇam*" is referred to in the epic.[70] Kṛṣṇa as a charioteer of Arjuna in the Great War of Kurukshetra is also mentioned.[71] The *Bhagavat Gītā* was also probably known to the people of the *Silappadikāram* period. According to V.R.R. Dikshitar, there is a reference to a *Gītā* verse in the *Varantharu Kāthai.*[72] *Silappadikāram* speaks of Kṛṣṇa as a divine flute player. The *Āycchiyar-Kuravai* verses describe him playing on the flute.[73] Here, three different adjectives are used for the flute, namely, *konrai, āmbal* and *mullai.* These names denote three different plants from which the instrument was made by the Tamils.[74] Perhaps these three names denote three different tunes —*paṇs* or *rāgas.* According to the commentator Adiarkunallar, these three terms refer to three ways of playing the flute.

Panchavīra Cult

The *Pāncharātra* school of the *Bhāgavata* cult seems to have made its advent in the South at least during the Sangam period. In *Puranānūru* Kṛṣṇa and Balarāma are described as Māyōn and Vāliyōn. Wherever Tirumāl is described in the Sangam works his elder brother Balarāma is also mentioned. While Māyōn is dark in colour, Vāliyōn is white. The former bears discus and *Garuda* flag and the latter has the plough and the palmyra in his hand. The fact that the Panchavīra cult of the *Bhāgavata* religion was well known to the Sangam works is very clear from a *Paripāḍal* verse which refers to the four *vyūha* forms of Viṣṇu.[75] It refers to the dark-complexioned Vāsudēva with red eyes (*sengatkāri*), the white-complexioned Baladēva with dark eyes (*karungkan veḷḷai*), the green-complexioned Pradyumna who was the son of Kṛṣṇa with golden eyes (*ponkaṭ patchai*) and Aniruddha Kṛṣṇa's grandson (*painkan-mā-al*). The above-mentioned heroes of the Vṛṣṇi clan were popular in North India well before 3rd century B.C. The same tradition had obviously spread to South India around 1st century B.C.

During the Sangam age, Kṛṣṇa and Balarāma had their own temples. This shows the popularity of the *Vyūha* forms or the *Panchavīra* cult. As it was in North of India, in South also, the *vyūha* phase of Viṣṇu worship was followed by the *vibhava* or *avatāra* phase. The *avatāra* concept was well known to the Sangam people. *Paripāḍal* says "God Tirumāl takes countless births in the course of the discharge of his threefold duties of creation, protection and destruction and he owes his creation to none."[76]

Archa or iconic form was also known to the Tamils of the Sangam period, though it was not so widespread. We get references to a few temples for Viṣṇu, Kṛṣṇa and Baladēva in the *Paripāḍal* and the *Silappadikāram.* A *Paripāḍal* verse[77] makes a special reference to the temple in Tirumāliruncholai (Alagarkōil near Madurai) dedicated to Kṛṣṇa and Balarāma. The author of this verse Ilamperuvaludiyār, a Pāṇḍya king, has beautifully described the hill Tirumalirun-cholaimalai. *Silappadikāram* refers to the temples of God Tirumāl at Madurai, Tirumaliruncholai,[78] and Kaveripūmpaṭṭinam;[79] separate temples for Balarāma are also mentioned in the epic.[80]

A poem of the *Paripāḍal* describes Tirumāl as one who could be recognised as an image by those who rely on the senses (naked eye); as the fire of the vēdic altar by vēdic scholars; as one present in the hearts of the yōgis and as one present everywhere by the sages. Another poem of the *Paripāḍal*[81] refers to the iconographic aspect of Lord Kṛṣṇa by saying that though the Lord is conceived of as having two arms, he is in reality having innumerable arms. Probably, the people of the later Sangam age worshipped the wooden images or the paintings of the Gods, kept in the temples. As part of the Panchavīra worship Kāma (Pradyumna), the son of Tirumāl, was popular among the Tamils during that time. Festivals were also celebrated in honour of Kāma during spring and summer seasons.[83] Image worship became more popular during the *Bhakti* movement in 7th-8th centuries A.D. The theistic ideas and sentiments seen in *Silappadikāram* and *Paripāḍal* anticipate those of the *Bhakti* movement and could very well be their forerunners.

Kṛṣṇa and the Pāṇḍyas of Madurai

The association of the Pāṇḍyas of Madurai with Kṛṣṇa and the Pāṇḍavas of the *Mahābhārata* fame is often mentioned in many ancient works. Greek writer Megasthenes gives a quaint account of Herakles (Kṛṣṇa) setting his daughter Pāṇḍaia to rule over the kingdom bordering on the southern sea. Megasthenes also says that her land was composed of 365 villages and each day one village brought its tribute to the royal household.[83] There is a similar statement in the Tamil epic *Silappadikāram* that on a particular day a certain cowherd family in a suburb of Madurai supplied ghee to the royal house.[84] The *Mahābhārata* mentions the rule of the Pāṇḍavas over the capital Kavatapura which is taken by some as Madurai and by some as an earlier capital.[85] Kātyāyana, the ancient grammarian (4th century B.C.), derives the name Pāṇḍyas from the clan of the Pāṇḍus. Interestingly, one of the names of the Pāṇḍyas that occur in the Sangam works is *Pancavar*, i.e. the five Pāṇḍava brothers.[86] Kanakasabai opines that the names of Pāṇḍyas and their capital city Madurai were derived from Pāṇḍavas and Mathura of North India respectively.[87] In fact, both the Sangam and the post-Sangam works mention the capital of the Pāṇḍyas as the "Southern Madurai" (*Ten Madurai*) and Mathura, the birth-place of Kṛṣṇa, is described in Tamil literature as "Northern-Madurai" (Vaḍa-Madurai) on the banks of the Yamunā.[88] There are also

4. Gōvardhanadhāri, Māmallapuram.

5. Gōvardhanadhāri, Māmallapuram.

6. Kāliya-mardana Kṛṣṇa, Māmallapuram.

7. Kudakkūttu (pot dance), Pundarikāksha Temple, Tiruvellarai.

8. Kṛṣṇa killing Bakāsura (bird), Tiruvellarai.

10. Kāliyamardana, Kāvēripakkam.

9. Vēnugōpāla, Kāvēripakkam.

14. Crawling Kṛṣṇa, Darasuram.

11. Vaṭapatrasāyi Kṛṣṇa, Vellore.

13. Yasoda-Kṛṣṇa, Chennai Museum.

12. Yasoda-Kṛṣṇa, Chennai Museum.

15. Crawling Kṛṣṇa images, Nayakaneripinyal (Tiruchi Dt.).

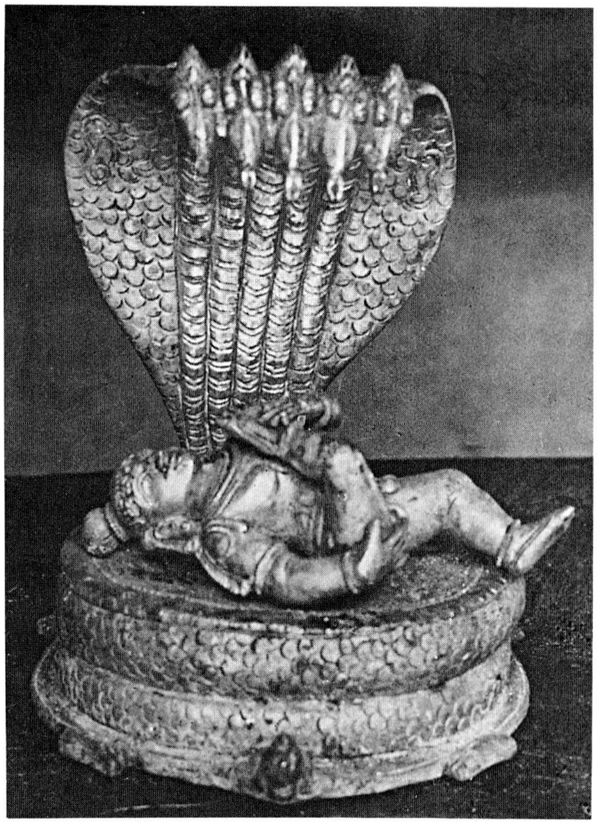

17. Santāna-Kṛṣṇa, Karaikoilpattu.

16. Crawling Kṛṣṇa, Ulundangudi.

18. Santāna-Kṛṣṇa, Chennai Museum.

19. Kṛṣṇa killing the elephant (Kuvalayāpiṭa), Tiruvendipuram.

21. Bakāsura-vadha, Sriperumbudur.

20. Kṛṣṇa killing the bird demon Bakāsura, Tiruvendipuram.

22. Bakāsura-vadha, Varadarajaswami Temple, Kanchi.

25. Navanīta-chora, Varadaraja Temple, Kānchi.

23. Gōvardhanadhāri-Kṛṣṇa, Kanchi.

27. Kṛṣṇa and Balarāma stealing butter, Vrinjipuram.

24. Navanīta-chora (Kṛṣṇa stealing butter), Tiruvendipuram.

26. Navanīta-chora, Tirukkunrungudi.

29. Kṛṣṇa undergoing punishment, Vellore.

28. Kṛṣṇa tied to the mortar, Kānchi.

30. Navanīta Kṛṣṇa, Seramādēvi.

31. Navanīta Kṛṣṇa, Satyamangalam.

32. Navanīta-Nritta Kṛṣṇa, Madurai.

33. Navanīta-Nritta Kṛṣṇa, Tirupuvanam.

34. Navanīta-Nritta Kṛṣṇa, Pallikonda.

35. Navanīta-Nritta Kṛṣṇa, Pallikonda.

36. Nardhana Kṛṣṇa in Chatura-tandava, Uttarakosamangai.

38. Kṛṣṇa in Chatura-tandava, Nerūr.

37. Nardhana Kṛṣṇa.

39. Nardhana-Kṛṣṇa.

40. Nardhana-Kṛṣṇa.

41. Nardhana-Kṛṣṇa.

42. Nardhana-Kṛṣṇa (sculpture), Srinivasanallur.

43. Kāliyanardhana, Sriperumbudur.

44. Kāliyanardhana, National Museum, New Delhi.

46. Kāliyanardhana, Tiruppullani.

45. Kāliyanardhana (Locality not known).

47. Kāliyanardhana, Thanjavur.

references to the participation of the Pāṇḍyas in the Kurukshetra war on the side of the Pāṇḍavas. The Pāṇḍyan kings from the 7th century repeatedly claim in their copper plates that they established the Tamil Sangam at Madurai and translated the *Mahābhāratam* in Tamil.[89]

Another interesting link between the Pāṇḍyas and Kṛṣṇa is found in the repeated references to the association of the former with a legendary ancestor Neḍiyōn. A verse in the *Puranānūru* extolls the Pāṇḍyan king (Palyāgasālai-mutu-kutumi-Peruvaḷudi) as having the noble qualities of Neḍiyōn.[90] Who was this Neḍiyōn? Some would take him to be a mythical ancestor. But there are many internal evidences to equate him with Viṣṇu or Kṛṣṇa. Another Sangam poem *Maduraikānchi* describes the Pāṇḍyan king as a descendant of "Nediyōn with the beautiful garland on his chest" which description is also given to Māyōn (Viṣṇu or Kṛṣṇa) in other Sangam poems.[91] The commentator Nacchinarkiniyār has identified Neḍiyōn with Kṛṣṇa at two places—one in his commentary on *MDK* and the other on *SLP*. The former extolls the Pāṇḍyan king as "a good teacher...like Neḍiyōn of great fortune who in himself has manifested all the worlds." The commentator identifies Neḍiyōn as Kṛṣṇa who was a teacher of the *Gītā* (Gītāchārya). Similarly, Neḍiyōn mentioned in the epic *SLP* is also identified as Kṛṣṇa by Nacchinarkiniyār.[92] Hardy F. who has discussed this point in great depth has brought in all references to Neḍiyōn and concludes: "The different ways of interpretation would point to the possibility that features of Neḍiyōn allude to Viṣṇu, Kṛṣṇa or Parasurāma (*malu-vāḷ-Neḍiyōn*), if he is not directly the God. If historical at all, this Neḍiyōn must have become a mythical figure for later generations who in various ways envisaged him in Vaiṣṇava terms."[93] In the *Kalithokai* and *Silappadikāram* we find references to the close association of the Pāṇḍyas with Māyōn (Kṛṣṇa). Many verses mention the praise of Māyōn and the welfare of the Pāṇḍyan king together.[94] One verse states: "Cowherds and their relations in whom the Pāṇḍyan king is firmly established"[95] indicating the association of the Pāṇḍyas with the cowherd clan. A verse composed by the Pāṇḍya king Kadalum-māinda Iḷam Peruvaludi is in praise of Kṛṣṇa and Balarāma whose abode was at Māl-irum-sōlai (i.e. Alagarmalai near Madurai).[96] A verse in the *SLP* says that the Pāṇḍyan king was none other than Kṛṣṇa.[97] The foregoing analysis of the Sangam works brings out clearly the close association of Kṛṣṇa with the Pāṇḍyan kings and their capital Madurai which had separate quarters for the cowherds (counterpart of Gōkulam near Mathura of north) who performed the *āichiyar-kuravai* dance.

Āy-Vēlirs and Kṛṣṇa

Another important line of chieftains of Tamilnāḍu during the Sangam period with whom Kṛṣṇa was intimately associated was the Āy-vēḷirs. The cowherds were known as *āyars* in Tamil even as they were known as Āhirs and Ābhiras in North India. Tradition says that the Āhirs in the Pāṇḍya country came to Tamilakam along with the ancestors of the Pāṇḍyas (*KLT*, verse 104: 4-6).[98] Potiya mountain region was known as Āy-kuḍi. The capital of that region is also called Āy-kuḍi. In his commentary on the prefatory *sūtra* to the *Tolkāppiyam*, Nacchinarkiniyār describes a tradition relating to the migration of the Yādava race as follows: The sage Agastya repaired to Dwārakā and taking with him 18 kings of the line of Kṛṣṇa, 18 families of Vēḷs or Vēḷirs and others, moved to the South with the Aruvāḷar tribes. There, he had the forests cleared and built up kingdoms settling therein all the people he had brought with him. Kapila, a poet probably of the 2nd century A.D., addresses the reigning Vēḷir chief as the 49th in descendence from the original founder of that dynasty.[99] M. Srinivasa Iyengar points out that allowing the usual 25 years for each generation, the above kingdom must have been established about B.C. 1075 and this may be assumed as the probable date of the migration of the Āy Vēḷirs to South India.[100] There were many Vēḷir chiefs in the Tamil country during the Sangam period. They had 'Āy' as a prefix or a suffix to their names, such as "Āy-andiran" and "Vēl-Āy". The latter had his capital in Āy-kuḍi and ruled the Potiya region. Many Sangam poets have glorified his bravery and charitable qualities. Poets like Uraiyūr Enichēri, Mudamōsiyār, Turaiyūr Ōdaikilar, Kūttuvan Kiranar, Umaṭṭur Kilanmaganār, Parankoṟṟanār, Paranar and Kārikannanar have composed poems in praise of this king and his region.

One of the Āykudi rulers was Āy-andiran. Once he defeated Kongars and drove them to western side.[101] A *Puranānūru* verse[102] says, "without the southern Āykudi the world will be in chaos". Pēgan, one of the Seven Vēlir chieftains (*Kaḍai-ēḷu-vaḷḷals*) of the Sangam period belonged to *Āviyar-kuḍi.* He was addressed by Kapilar as '*Āviyar Kōve*'.[103]

M. Raghava Iyengar held that the popularity of the worship of Kṛṣṇa in the ancient Tamiḷakam might be partly due to the influence of the Vēḷirs who are often referred to in the Sangam works. He has clearly shown that the Vēḷirs referred to in the Sangam works belonged to the 18 Kuḍi-vēḷirs of the descendants of the Yadu-kula to which Kṛṣṇa also belonged, and that the Vēḷirs migrated from Dwarapati, and settled in different parts of South India.[104] The Āy-Vēḷir kings of later period also mention in their copper plate charters that they belonged to the Yadu-kula of Kṛṣṇa.

The Āy dominion was situated between Kerala and Pāṇḍya Nāḍu and it comprised of the parts of the present Kanyakumari district of Tamilnāḍu. The Sangam literature portrays the Āy rulers as independent sovereigns in the region around Potiya hill. The early Āys hold special position among the Vēḷir chieftains ruling in several parts of the Tamil country. The

Parthivasekarapuram inscription of Kōkkurunandakkan—the Āy ruler—claims that he belonged to the line of the Yādavas or Āyar.

People who lived in the *mullai* region were called as *āyars*, *kōyalars* and *idayars*. In Tamil land division *mullai* is placed in the mid-region between the hills (*kurinchi*) and the plains (*marudam*). As *mullai* enjoys the *iḍai* (middle) position, the people of that region were called *Iḍaiyars*. There are references to *Iḍaiyars* in the Sangam works.[105] The name of one of the poets was *Iḍaikkadanar*. The name denotes that the poet belonged to *mullai* region. Even now *iḍaiyar* is the most commonly used word for the cowherds in Tamil. According to the *Tolkāppiyam*, the presiding deity of the *mullai* region was Māyōn i.e. Kṛṣṇa or Viṣṇu. Another name for the āyars was *pothuvar*,[106] meaning 'common', We have reference to *pothuvar* in the *Kalithokai*.[107]

The Āy kings continued to cherish their association with Yadu-kula and Kṛṣṇa in the later times also as seen in their copper plate grants and inscriptions. This will be discussed in greater detail in a later chapter.

Myths of Kṛṣṇa Special to Sangam Literature

We have so far reviewed how the Sangam works reveal the assimilation of Viṣṇu worship with the allied doctrines of *vyūha* and *avatāra* concepts found in the Sanskrit texts of North India. Particularly they show how the Kṛṣṇa cult was completely identified with Viṣṇu in Tamil regions. As we have already seen, the Pāncharātra concepts of *vyūha* and *avatāra* were well-known tenets in Tamilakam during the Sangam and the post-Sangam period.

But there are references to some episodes (from Kṛṣṇa's life) which cannot be traced back to Sanskrit literature. Peculiar qualities were attributed to Kṛṣṇa and many new myths and religious attitudes were recorded for the first time in the Sangam works. While many of the Kṛṣṇāyaṇa stories which found mention in the ancient Tamil works could have been the result of the influence of the Sanskrit literature, some other themes and episodes seem to be of indigenous origin and have no precedent or parallel.

The *Puranānūru* gives a detailed account of a miracle performed by Māyōn. It says: when the Asuras had hidden away the sun and plunged the whole world into darkness, the dark-complexioned God rescued the sun, placed him on the sky and thus protected the mankind.[108] This legend, according to many scholars, is not directly traceable to the Sanskrit works.

The *Ahanānūru* gives a detailed account of *vastrāpaharaṇa* episode with some interesting changes. The verse says: when the cowherd girls were taking bath, Kṛṣṇa took all their clothes and climbed the *Kurunda* tree. He saw Balarāma approaching the spot and at once bent a branch of the tree in order to hide the Gopis from his brother. After Balarāma had gone, he gave back the clothes to the girls.[109] This version of the *vastrāpaharaṇa* episode is not to be seen in any of the Sanskrit works. In the *BGP* version Balarāma does not figure in this episode. The introduction of Balarāma in the episode is peculiar to Tamil tradition.

Another example is provided by the *Kuravai* dance. According to Tamil tradition, Kṛṣṇa and Balarāma were inseparable. This might have been due to the influence of *Vyūha* concept. After the post-Sangam period when the *avatāra* concept became more popular than the *Vyūha*, Balarāma lost his place of importance. During the Bhakti period the Āḻvārs did not pay much attention to Balarāma.

Another childhood prank of Kṛṣṇa is referred to in the *SLP* which says: when Kṛṣṇa was sporting in the waters of Yamunā with the Gōpis, he took away a bracelet from one of them and teased them.[110]

Many customs and traditions which are peculiar to Tamil country and particularly to the cowherd community are attributed to Kṛṣṇa. A verse in *Kalithokai*[111] says that an Āy girl would not marry the man who was afraid to face a bull fight. This shows that "it was a custom in the cowherd community for young girls, until they were married, to select their own bulls from the common stall and to tend them. The bulls would then be let loose, and whichever young cowherd could successfully bring the beast under control in an open contest, was deemed the proper life-partner for the girl. Apparently, it was one of the ancient wedding customs of the Āyars. This custom also can be traced to their family deity Kṛṣṇa, who curbed the fury of seven bulls coloured black, white and brown and married the girls who were tending them."[112] Hardy says: "Thus we have here the document of the Tamil south envisaging the Northern God Kṛṣṇa within the confines of its own customs."[113]

The introduction of Nappinnai as Kṛṣṇa's spouse is another special feature of southern Kṛṣṇaism. No mention was made regarding Nappinnai in Sanskrit literature. Nappinnai or Pinnai enjoys a very important position in Kṛṣṇa's life as far as Tamil works are concerned. Some scholars are of the opinion that Pinnai was a counterpart of Rādhā of North India.[114] According to them in the Sanskrit sources Rādhā figures only after the 10th century as the favourite *gopi* of Kṛṣṇa. Tamil works like the *Silappadikāram* and the *Maṇimēkalai* mention that Kṛṣṇa married Pinnai in the traditional manner of *Āyarkudi* i.e. after a hard bull baiting contest in which Kṛṣṇa subdued seven bulls. The post-Sangam works like *Silappadikāram, Maṇimēkalai* and *Eighteenkīlkanakku* provide us with information about Pinnai. So, some scholars are of the opinion that the Nappinnai cult developed in Tamilnāḍu. But it continued to be popular even during the Bhakti period. It is quite likely that it became the forerunner and a source of inspiration for the cult of Rādhā in

North India when the southern Bhakti movement influenced North India.

SLP says: "We shall sing of the charming beauty of Pinnai as she danced with her husband on the banks of Yamunā."[115] Along with Pinnai, a new dance form named "*kuravai*" was also introduced. Obviously, it was a custom of the Āyars of Tamilakam to perform dance as a group. *Maṇimēkalai* refers to the *kuravai* dance performed by Kṛṣṇa along with Pinnai and Baladēva.[116] Kṛṣṇa's love for Pinnai was so great that he became indifferent to *Srī*. The *SLP* says, "She who garlanded Māyāvan with the luxurious *tulasi* garland would perform the faultless *kuravai* dance. Is Pinnai of bangled arms so beautiful that he who had won great reputation by measuring the universe, would not look at Lakshmi, dwelling in his own breast?"

SLP says, "Among the many boyhood games played by Kṛṣṇa and Balarāma in the Ayarpāḍi, *Kuravai* was one."[117] If we look into the sources for this *Kuravai* dance, many interesting facts are revealed. *Viṣṇu Purāṇa* speaks about a dance form similar to *rāsa-krīḍā*. But it differs from the *Kuravai* in the sense that Balarāma was completely missing in the *rāsa* dance while he always accompanied Kṛṣṇa and Pinnai in the *Kuravai* dance. Hardy thoroughly deals with the origin of the dance form. His arguments are based on verse 3 in *Āycchiyarkuravai* of the epic *Silappadikāram*. The translation runs like this, "Let us dance the *Kuravai* which Māyāvan danced together with Pinnai...which is among the dances of the *Vālacaritai* which were danced by him and his elder brother...in Vraja." According to Hardy, *Hallisaka* dance form is described in the *Bālacharita* of Bhāsa. It was danced by Kṛṣṇa and his elder brother Balarāma. A very similar dance form has also been mentioned in Bhāsa's drama *Pāncharātra*. Hardy claims that the *Vālacaritai* mentioned in the verse is none other than the *Bālacharita* of Bhāsa. "We are thus dealing here with a definite source of southern Kṛṣṇa myth. Also the *Kuravai* is danced by Kṛṣṇa and his elder brother, and the *āycchiyar* dance is an apotropaic ritual (which indicates a merger of the very similar dances described in the *Bālacharita* and *Pāncharātra*)...Since Bhāsa has been dated to 3rd or 4th century A.D. this would constitute the *terminas aquo* for the introduction of the myth into the south, and by assuming the 6th century or so as the date of the renaissance works this would indeed allow for a period of about two centuries during which the myth developed along typically southern lines."[118]

The cowherd girls used to draw a circle on the floor and divide it into twelve rooms. Seven dancing girls were made to stand in these rooms and were named as *kural, tuttam, kaikilai, uzai, ili, vilari, taram.* They denote the seven notes of the musical scale. They also refer to seven *paṇṇs.* These dancing girls used to play the parts of Māyāvan, Pinnai and Balarāma and enacted the episodes from the life of Kṛṣṇa.[119]

One of the earliest literary references to Kṛṣṇa as a dancer (apart from the *rāsa* dance) also occurs in Tamil literature. From the Sangam collection we get the description of the eleven dance forms, namely, *alliyam, koṭṭi, kuḍam, kuḍai, mallāḍal, pandurangam, thuḍi, pēḍu, marakkāl, pāvai* and *kaḍayam.* Of the above eleven, five dance forms are said to have been performed in Bāṇa's city by Kṛṣṇa, Pradyumna and Lakshmi. Of these dances we come to know about three dance forms from the *Silappadikāram:*[120]

1) *Alliyam* performed by Kṛṣṇa after killing the elephant Kuvalayāpita employed by Kamsa.[121]

2) *Mallāḍal* performed by Kṛṣṇa after killing the demon Bāṇa.[122]

3) *Kuḍakkūttu.* This pot dance was performed by Kṛṣṇa in the streets of So, the city of Bāṇāsura, in order to rescue Aniruddha who was imprisoned by the former when the latter wanted to marry Uṣa, the daughter of Bāṇāsura.[123]

The *Paripāḍal* refers to Kṛṣṇa's dance forms such as *Kuravai* and *Kuḍam.* It says that Kṛṣṇa performed *Kuḍakkūttu* dance keeping pots on the head and the shoulders.[124] The dancer would balance a pile of pots on his head, and a few more on his shoulders and throw up some pots in the air and catch them as they fall one by one, thus keeping a continuous line of pots going round.

It could have also been performed in a different way. The dancer would have only one pot and without touching it with his hands, only with the movement of muscles, he would move the pot gradually from head to neck, then to shoulder, from there to the arms and back again. This *kuḍam* dance very much resembled the present-day *karagam* dance, a folk dance of Tamilnāḍu.

This concept of Kṛṣṇa as a heroic dancer is rather missing in the Northern texts. Kṛṣṇa as a dancer in *rāsa krīḍā* developed very late in the north though the *rāsa* dance is referred to in the *Viṣṇu Purāṇa.* The *rāsa* dance pictured Kṛṣṇa as youth when he was romantically involved with cowherd girls. The *rāsa-krīḍā* dance emphasises the aspect of Kṛṣṇa as a lover of Gōpis. But on the other hand, the dance forms referred to in the Tamil literature had nothing to do with Gōpis or eroticism. *Alliyam, mallāḍal* and *kuḍam* all these stress Kṛṣṇa's heroism and bravery. Each one of them was associated with a heroic deed of Kṛṣṇa. These instances illustrate how the Kṛṣṇa life-stories were adapted and absorbed into the Tamil cultural milieu.

We see another interesting instance of the adaptation in the depiction of Durgā (Kotravai) in the *SLP.* According to the *MBH* Durgā was the sister of Kṛṣṇa. But the Tamil epic goes a step further and attributes some of the feats of Kṛṣṇa to her, like the killing of the wheel-demon (Sakaṭāsura).

Thus, we see that the ancient Tamil Sangam classics provide a rich store of very valuable information on the advent and growth of the Kṛṣṇa cult in

Tamilnāḍu and the process of its adaptation and assimilation into the Tamil cultural and religious ethos.

References

1. Hardy, F., *Viraha-Bhakti*, p. 19. "The central event of the epic (*MBH*) viz. the struggle between the Kauravas and Pāṇḍavas may be regarded as historical...and may be approximately dated at about 1000 B.C." R.C. Mazumdar, *Ancient India* (1960), p. 72.

1a. *RV*, VIII.85.13-15.

2. *RV*, *ibid.* Tr. Griffith.

3. *RV*, I.116-23.

   I.117-7. Tr. Griffith.

   RV, VIII.84.3-4. For a detailed discussion on Vedic reference to Kṛṣṇa, see B. Preciado-Solis, *The Kṛṣṇa Cycle in the Purāṇas* (1984).

4. *Chāndōgya Upanishad*, III.17, 6.

5. Raychaudhuri, *Early History of the Vaiṣṇava Sect*, p. 57.

6. *RV*, III.53.7.

7. *VSMRS*, p. 10.

8. Sircar, *R.L.A.M.I.*, p. 26.

9. Banerjee, P., *Life of Krishna in Indian Art*, p. 7.

10. Hardy, F., *Viraha-Bhakti*, p. 20, fn. 33.

11. Barnett, *Hindu Gods and Heroes*, p. 92.

12. Macdonell, A.A., *History of Sanskrit Literature*, p. 17.

    Basham, A.L., *The Wonder that was India*, p. 164.

13. *Taittiriya Samhitā*, III.11.9.3.

    Taittiriya Brāhmaṇa, III.10.9.15.

    Satapata Brāhmaṇa, III.1.1.4.

    Jaiminiya Upanishad, I.6.1.

14. *Pāṇini Sūtra*, II.2.23.

15. Sen, D.N., *Select Inscriptions—Garuda Pillar at Bedsa.*

16. *Cultural Heritage of India* (R.K. Mission Pub.), Vol. IV, p. 117.

17. *MBH*, V.20; 47.

18. *MBH*, I.1, 103.

19. *MBH*, VI.66.31-41.

20. *RV*, VI, 22, 16-17.

21. *RV*, VI, 2.5. 2-3.

22. *Epigraphia Indica*, Vol. X, Inscription No. 669.

23. *Dharmasamsthābanārthāya Sambavāmi vuge yuge* (B.G.).

23a. *Op. cit.*, p. 16.

24. R.G. Bhandarkar, *VSMRS.*

25. *RV*, V.52, 17.

26. *RV,* I.22.18; X.19.4.
27. *RV,* I.154-6.
28. Gonda, J., *Aspects of Early Vishnuism,* pp. 1-11.
29. Sen, Sukumar, *A History of Brajabhumi Lit.,* p. 480.
30. Schulberg, Lucilee, *Historic India,* p. 128.
31. *RV,* III.36.9; X.184.1; III.54.14.
32. Singer, Milton, *Krishna: Myths, Rites and Attitudes,* p. 182.
    A.L. Basham for the date of this work, *op. cit.,* p. 461.
33. Morgan, K.W., *Religion of the Hindus,* p. 41.
34. Banerjea, J.N., *The Development of Hindu Iconography,* p. 208.
35. Mazumdar, R.C., *Classical Age,* p. 422.
36. *Tolkāppiyam Porulatikaram,* 5.
37. *Naṟṟinai.*
38. *Madurai-Kānchi,* 590-599.
39. *Kalithokai,* V.52; 1-5.
40. "*Kanru Kunilāy erinda Māyavan*"—*Silap.*
41. Dikshitar, V.R.R., *Silappadikāram,* p. 234.
42. Iyengar, M. Raghava, "*Araycchi-thoguti*", p. 53.
43. *PRP,* 15.1.49-50.
44. Sanjivi, N., *Sanga Ilakkiya Āraycchi Aṭṭavanai,* pp. 21-22.
45. Marr, J.R., *The Eight Anthologies* (1985), p. 389.
46. *PRP,* verse 1, lines 31-33.
47. Iyengar, S.K., *Religion of the Tamils of Sangam Age,* p. xiii.
48. *Panai kodiyōnum, mannuru tirumani purayum mēni, vinnuvir putkoḍi.*
49. *PRN,* 56.
50. *PRN,* 58, *Panai kodiyōnum nīlnira uravin nemiyōnum enru iruperuntheyyamum.*
51. *PRN,* 57:1-3.

51a. *MDK,* 761-763.

52. *AHN,* 59.
53. *KLT,* 105:9-12.
54. *KLT,* V.103:11:53-55:
    Mevār vitutta kūnthar kuthinainathu vāy pukuthitherputaitha.
55. *PRP,* V.3; 11.31-32.
56. *KLT,* V.134.
57. *Kali,* V.104-111.
58. *Iru nilam kadanta tirumarumārbin munnīr vaṇṇan* (1.402).
59. *Perum,* 11.480-485.
60. *MDK,* 590-599.
61. *SLP,* XVII.V.33, 1-3.
62. *Ibid.,* V.19.1.1:
    Kannu kunilāy kani udhirtha māyavan.

63. *Ibid.*, V.21:1.1:

    kollayam sāral kurunthositha māyavan.

64. *Ibid.*, V.23.11.1-2:

    Iru men sāyal nudanga nudangi aruvai oḷinthḷ.

65. *Ibid.*, V.32.1-3:

    Kalakkiya kai asōdaiyār kadaikayiṟṟāl kāṭṭun kai.

66. *SLP*, XVII.V.26; 1-1:

    Kathir thikiriyōn maraitha kadal vaṇṇan.

67. *Ibid.*, 34:1-3; 37-11:2-4:

    Natanthavadi panchayarku thūthaka natantha aḍi.

68. *Ibid.*, V.37, 11.1-3.

69. *SLP*, XVII.V.29:

    Kōyāmalai āram kōtta kadalāram; Devarkōn punāram thevar kōn marbinane; Devarkōn pūnāram pūndan chezundu vana gōkulam mēythu kurunthosithan enbavaral.

70. *SLP*, 2.17.1.23.

71. *SLP*, 1.17.1.34.

72. Dikshitar, V.R.R., *Silappadikāram*, p. 342.

73. *SLP*, Āycchiyar Kuravai.

74. Commentary of Adiyārku Nallār.

75. *PRP*, V.3, 11.81-82:

    Sengatkāri karungkan veḷḷai ponkat patchai paingkan mā āl.

76. *PRP*, V.3, 71.-72.

77. *PRP*, V.15, 10-14.

78. *SLP*, XI.11.91:

    Tirumāl kunrattu chelguvir āyin.

79. *SLP*, X.11:9-10:

    Anikilar aravin arituyil amarnda maṇivaṇṇan kōṭṭam.

80. *SLP*, V.1.171; IX.1.10.

81. *PRP*, 3-4.35-45.

82. *KLT*, V.27. 1-24; V.92, 1-67.

83. McCrindle, *Ancient India as described by Megasthenes and Arrian*, pp. 163-164.

84. *SLP*, 17-5-2.

85. *MBH*, VII.11-398; VII.23.

86. *Perum*, 58-8.

87. Kanakasabai, V., *Tamils 1800 Years Ago*, pp. 23-25. He is of the view that the Pāṇḍus of the north established their rule in the south at Madurai.

88. Āṇḍāḷ in her *Tiruppāvai* describes Kṛṣṇa as one born in North Madurai on the banks of the Yamunā (Vadamadurai maindan and Yamunai turaivan (V.5).

89. *Madurāpuri-sangamvaittu mābhāratam Tamil Paḍutti* (Dalavāyapuram and Larger Sinnamanur copper plates).

90. *Perum*, 9:8-11.

91. *MDK*, 61 and 763.
92. *Ibid.*, 763; Hardy, *op. cit.*, p. 616.
93. Hardy, *op. cit.*, p. 612.
94. *Kali*, 46-50; 70-75; 77-80 etc.
95. *Kali*, 105, 1-7.
96. *SLP*, XVII.V.29. It also adds the Chēra and the Chōḷa kings were none but Viṣṇu.
97. *Paripādal*, V.15.
98. Kanakasabai, *Tamils 1800 Years Ago*, p. 109.
99. *PRN*, 201: *Uvarā vikaittuvarai vāndunarpathonpatu vazimurai vantha velirul vela.*
100. Aiyangar, M. Srinivasa, *Tamil Studies*, pp. 45-46.
101. *PRN*, 130.
102. *PRN*, 132: *Thenthisai āykudi inrayin ivulakame nilai pirazum.*
103. *PRN*, 147.
104. Iyengar, M. Raghava, *Vēḷir Varalāru.*
105. *PRN*, 54: *Masun udukkai maḍivāy iḍaiyan sirathalai āyamodu kurugal chella.*
106. Pillai, Auvai S. Duraisami, *Ainkurunūru.*
107. *KLT*, 103.
108. *PRN*, 174:1-5.
109. *AHN*, 59. A similar version is found in the Tamil epic *Jīvaka Chintāmani* (V.209).
110. *SLP*, 2.17.11.23-24.
111. *KLT*, 103:63-64.
112. Dikshitar, V.R.R., *Silappadikāram*, p. 230.
113. Hardy, F., *Viraha-Bhakti*, p. 197.
114. Dikshitar, V.R.R., *op. cit.*
115. *Silappadikāram, Āir kuravai.*
116. *Manimekalai*, XIX.11.65-66:
Māmanivannanum thamunum
Pinnaiyum āḍiya kuravayil
Thām ena nōkkiyum.
117. *SLP*, *Āychhiyarkuravai*, 3.
118. Hardy, F., *op. cit.*, pp. 198-199.
By Tamil renaissance works Hardy means *SLP*, *KLT* and a late poem in the *AHN*.
119. Souri, *Inthia Kalayum Kalacharamum*, p. 4.
120. *SLP*, Canto VI.L. 4616.
121. *SLP*, VI.11:46-48:
Kanchan vancham kadattatharkāka
Anjanavannan ādiya adalul thokuthiyum.
122. *SLP*, V.11:48-49: *Avunar kadantha mallalin ādalum.*
123. *SLP*, VI.11:54-55.
124. *PRP*, .3:1-83.

Chapter II

KṚṢṆA IN THE TAMIL BHAKTI TRADITION

Introduction

The Bhāgavata movement centring around Kṛṣṇa had its origin in the Mathura region and reached its high point during the Gupta age (4th century A.D.), when it flowered into a full-fledged Bhāgavata cult leading to a broad-based worship of the Brahmanical deities, and in particular, Viṣṇu and his various incarnations (*avatāras*). This was also the age when the *Purāṇas* were codified and according to several scholars, the *Viṣṇu Purāṇa* was composed during this period. The Purāṇas served as the vehicle for popularising the theistic form of worship through the various legends and myths connected with the Brahmanical deities. The myths connected with Viṣṇu worship were elaborated in the *Viṣṇu Purāṇa, Kūrma Purāṇa, Varāha Purāṇa,* etc. They served the same purpose as the Jātaka stories and the stories connected with Buddha's life which were elaborately carved in the Buddhist centres such as Sanchi, Saranath and Barhut. From the Gupta period, we also see beautiful sculptural representations of the purāṇic episodes connected with Viṣṇu and Siva. Well-known examples are to be found in the Gupta temples like the Dasāvatāra temple at Deogarh. The gigantic figure of Bhūvarāha in the Udayagiri caves in Madhya Pradesh is an outstanding example to show the greatness of Viṣṇu, clearly indicating the growing popularity of the Brahmanical deities and in particular Viṣṇu and his manifestations. It is significant also to note that the Gupta kings proclaimed themselves as *Parama Bhāgavatas* and scholars are generally agreed that they were responsible for popularising the Bhāgavata cult in different parts of North India. This tradition that was set in motion by the Guptas had certainly influenced the Deccan and South India. We see the kings of South India like the Chālukyas of Bādami and the Pallavas of Kānchi and the Pāṇḍyas of Madurai adopting Sanskrit in their official documents like their copper plates more or less on the same pattern set by the Gupta kings. Interestingly enough we find strikingly similar passages and *birudas* or titles in their copper plates too. We see both the Pallava and Pāṇḍya kings calling themselves as *Parama Bhāgavatas* and *Parama Māheśwaras* in line with the Gupta classical tradition and identifying themselves with the movement.

The Pallava period particularly from the 6th century A.D. onwards coincided with the Bhakti movement in Tamilnāḍu and it was indeed a turning point in the religious and art history of Tamilnāḍu. It was during this period that this movement championed by the Tamil poet-saints became very popular. Perhaps nowhere else in India did this devotional upsurge take such an intense form in this period as it did in Tamilnāḍu. There were some special reasons for this. One of them was the Kaḷabhra interregnum that preceded this for about 100 years and brought about widespread disturbances and unrest in the social and religious life of Tamilnāḍu. We get clear references to the hostile activities of the Kaḷabhras against the Vēdic religion and Vēdic establishments in the contemporary literature and also inscriptions. The Vēḷvikuḍi grant of the Pāṇḍyas (8th century A.D.) describes Kaḍungōn of the Pāṇḍya line as one who liberated the Pāṇḍya country from the clutches of the Kaḷabhras and emerged as a resplendent sun from the dark clouds of the Kaḷabhras.[1] Similar sentiments are found in the Pallava copper plates giving the credit to Simha Viṣṇu as a vanquisher of the Kaḷabhras. There is still dispute among the scholars regarding the identification of the Kaḷabhras.[2] But recent researches, based on epigraphical and literary evidences, tend to identify them as a fanatical Jaina group, very hostile to the Vēdic institutions and rituals which entrenched itself strongly in some places of Tamilnāḍu. In fact, the Vēḷvikuḍi grant mentioned above makes a pointed reference to the confiscation of the lands granted to a set of Brahmins by an earlier Pāṇḍya king. After the elimination of the Kaḷabhras, the descendants of that family approached the Pāṇḍya king (Nedunchadaiyan Parāntaka) and told him of injustice done to them by the Kaḷabhras and requested the king to re-grant the lands to them, which the king did. All these facts clearly show the disturbed social conditions in which the new line of the Pāṇḍyas took over the reins of the government and the significance of the terms '*Parama Bhāgavatas*' and '*Parama Māheśwaras*'.

It is against the same background that we have to look at the Bhakti movement of Tamilnāḍu as well. The activities of the Kaḷabhras provoked a strong reaction which was given expression to in the hymns of the Āḷvārs and Nāyanmārs. We see in their works repeated condemnation of Jainas and the Buddhists. In the works of Jnānasambandhar in particular, we get vivid descriptions of Jainas wandering about naked with their dishevelled hair which, according to him, was revolting. Repeatedly, they plead to the people to reject the heterodox religions as something against our own cultural heritage and turn to our age-old Vēdic and Purāṇic gods like Viṣṇu and Siva. We see in the works of Vaiṣṇava Āḷvārs the forthright rejection of Buddhism and Jainism and the glorification of Viṣṇu as the supreme deity.

The Āḷvārs wanted to revive Viṣṇu worship and Vaiṣṇava religion but not with the old methods of rituals and sacrifices which came under great criticism from the Buddhists and Jainas. They did it by a very distinctly modified form with the emphasis on love and devotion for salvation.[3]

The essential characteristics of their approach can be summed up as follows:

Bhakti

Bhakti or devotion to a personal and lovable God was a dominant theme, as against impersonal and abstract divinities. They projected the Hindu divinities as intensely human, partaking in the joys and sorrows of their fellow men. An example was that of Kṛṣṇa and his intimate relationship with the Pāṇḍavas for whose sake he underwent many trials and tribulations. They described God as a friend, philosopher and guide. The personality of Kṛṣṇa came in very handy to show these qualities.

The Idol and the Temple

The *archā* or idol form as a concrete, visible object full of beauty to which a common man can perform *pūjā, abhishēka,* offer food and flower and concentrate his devotion is emphasised. They described it as '*archāvatāra*' (idol incarnation). Hand in hand with this idea goes the institution of temple which is inseparable from the idol as the abode of the Lord. Repeatedly, the Āḷvārs mention that the idol in the temple is none other than the *Vēda puruṣa,*[4] thus reconciling the ancient Vēdic worship with the newly emerging institution, namely, the temple. Implied in this was also the important idea that the elaborate Vēdic rituals were unnecessary and avoidable and what was required was a sincere and true devotion (*Bhakti*) or even self-surrender (*Prapatti*). The Vaiṣṇava teachers (*āchāryas*) who followed the Āḷvārs have stated that the Āḷvārs preached the path of surrender (*Prapatti-mārga* or *Saraṇāgati-tatva*) as set out by Kṛṣṇa in the *Bhagavat Gītā* in the last verse (*Carama-slōka*). According to them, the *prapatti-mārga* is a further simplification of the mode of worship. Even the humblest and the lowliest, indeed even the animal—the elephant (Gajēndra in the Gajēndra-mōksha story), could have direct access to the Lord by a simple self-surrender. There was no need of a priest or a ceremony.[5]

Purāṇic Allusion

Another interesting feature of their hymns is the repeated allusion to the *purāṇic* lore centring around Viṣṇu and his different manifestations or *avatāras* and localisation of myths. Obviously, it was the means by which they could present the extraordinary and divine deeds of the Lord to the common masses and bring the purāṇic lore within their easy access. Their poems reveal an intimate knowledge of even the obscure episodes mentioned in the Purāṇas and the epics. In fact, some of the episodes not mentioned in the Purāṇas are to be found in the Āḷvārs' hymns. This will be discussed further later on.

Liberal Attitude towards the Caste System

Hailing from different strata of society, their language carried conviction and in a number of places, they state that for a true Bhāgavata, there was no caste barrier. In one of the most famous verses, Toṇḍaradipoḍi, a Brahmin saint, states that the true devotees of Viṣṇu or the Bhāgavatas, even if they belonged to the outcaste, are worthy of our highest veneration.[6] On the contrary, if a Brahmin steeped in the Four Vēdas were to offend a true devotee of a lower caste, he himself should be treated as an outcaste. In particular, the Kṛṣṇa story became a favourite theme in this context. Periāḷvār, another Brahmin saint, said: "We will forsake our old castes and become members of one large community serving God."[6a]

Easy Accessibility of the Lord (Saulabhya)

Kṛṣṇa who had a humble origin of the cowherd clan became their favourite. Incidents like stealing the butter, allowing himself to be tied up and beaten and his role as a charioteer of Arjuna are often mentioned to illustrate the great quality of his easy accessibility. Many-faceted character of Kṛṣṇa was a boon to the Āḷvārs both for their personal experience and devotion and also to project his many aspects as a vehicle to popularise Vaiṣṇavism. Kṛṣṇa's story answered all the requirements of the Āḷvārs. It gave ample scope for expressing their mystic experiences. The mischievous but lovable feats of the cowherd boy, first described in the *Viṣṇu Purāṇa*, were elaborated with great devotion and feeling by the Āḷvārs. They in all probability formed the source of inspiration for the *Bhāgavata Purāṇa*. According to many scholars, the *purāṇa* was written in Tamilnāḍu in the post-Bhakti period (9th century A.D.).

Language—Tamil

The saints used simple and mellifluous Tamil language to express their experiences and sentiments and not only drew upon the ancient Tamil Sangam classics but also introduced new forms oriented towards the Bhakti or emotional devotion.

As a divine child, as a romantic youth, as a statesman and as a teacher of the great *Bhagavat Gītā* Kṛṣṇa's versatile and charismatic personality was the most appropriate to be projected as a supreme God. The Tamil names used by the Āḷvārs to denote the versatility of Kṛṣṇa's character are highly significant:

Kaṇṇan (the one with beautiful (lotus) eyes; also the darling)

Āyar-Koḷundu (the tender sprout of the cowherd clan)

Āyar kula-aniviḷakku (the leading light of the cowherd community)

Māyan (the great dissembler; the inscrutable)

Mugil-vaṇṇan (one whose colour is that of the clouds)

Neḍiyōn (who is immeasurable)

Kūttan (the dancer; *māyakkūttan,* the divine dancer)

Kaḷvan (the thief of the butter and our hearts)

Tēr-pākan (the charioteer)

Panchavar-tūtan (the messenger of the Five (the Pāṇḍavas))

Jnānachiru-kuḷavi (a child of profound wisdom)

Tamil as their medium of expression, the Āḷvārs had an advantage of directly appealing to the masses in their own language. The stories of the *Purāṇas,* and the philosophical ideas which were in Sanskrit were retold by them in simple and beautiful Tamil. It had a remarkable effect on the Tamil society.

We shall see in the forthcoming pages how the Āḷvārs drew upon the Kṛṣṇa theme to the full extent and gave a new dimension to it with their own experiences and poetic imagination. Some of them took the role of the mother, some as a friend and a lover (*gōpikā*) and some others treated him as the supreme God. The experience varies from one Āḷvār to another, each one of them surpassing the other. All these went to make the rich Kṛṣṇa lore in the Tamil Bhakti literature which became a source of inspiration for the later Vaiṣṇava preceptors like Yāmuna and Rāmānuja and through them several other Bhakti schools all over India.

The First Three Āḷvārs

Poikai, Bhūtam and Pēy are together known as Mudalāḷvārs (The First Āḷvārs). Their birth-places were Kānchi, Kaḍal-mallai (Mahabalipuram) and Mailai (Mylapore) respectively. They all belonged to Toṇḍaināḍu and they met one another in a small corridor of a Viṣṇu temple at Thirukkōvalūr in South Arcot district and burst forth in spontaneous ecstasy and sang 100 verses each in praise of Lord Viṣṇu. Their historic meeting is regarded as marking the commencement of the Bhakti movement in Tamilnāḍu by the Vaiṣṇavas. Historians place the three early saints around 600 A.D.

Majority of their poems glorify the Lord of Seven Hills (Vēnkaḍam) who is addressed as Kṛṣṇa, Rāma and Viṣṇu. They attribute the exploits of Kṛṣṇa to the Lord of Vēnkaḍam. Poikaiāḷvār attributes the Govardhana hill episode to the Lord of Thiruvenkaḍam.[7] He also says that we can worship Kṛṣṇa who subjugated seven bulls in Vēnkaḍam.[8] The other exploits of Kṛṣṇa like stealing the butter, killing Kamsa, killing the elephant-demon, Bakasura-vadha, breaking of the *Maruda* tree, bending the *Kurunda* tree and hiding the sun with a wheel of the chariot during the *Mahābhārata* war—all occur in his hymns. He describes Thirukkōvalūr as the place where Kṛṣṇa is said to have grazed the cows.[9] Kōvala is the Tamil equivalent of the Sanskrit word Gopāla.

Bhūtattāḷvār has sung many verses in praise of the Lord of Vēnkatam and Srirangam. He attributes many exploits of Kṛṣṇa to them. Pūtana-vadha, Kṛṣṇa as a charioteer, Chakaṭāsura-vadha, the subjugation of seven bulls to wed Pinnai, killing of Kamsa and Kuḍam-dance are the exploits of Kṛṣṇa mentioned by Bhūtattāḷvār.[10] The Āḷvār says, "The Lord of Thiruvenkatam and the Lord of Srirangam are none other than Kṛṣṇa, who killed the elephant Kuvalayāpita."[11]

Pēyāḷvār born in Mylapore in Madras has sung about Kṛṣṇa as Pārthasārathi of Triplicane.[12] He sees in Kṛṣṇa a combination of mighty power and submissiveness—the former against his enemies as in the Bhārata war for the sake of the Pāṇḍavas and the latter before his friends and devotees as when he permitted himself to be beaten by the churning rod of his mother. Many other exploits of Kṛṣṇa as a child are also mentioned by him.[13]

Tirumaḷisai-āḷvār, born in Tirumaḷisai near Poondamalli about 30 km from Chennai city, was probably a younger contemporary of the Mudalāḷvārs. He has two works to his credit. They are *Nānmukan-Tiruvantāti* and *Tiruchanda-Viruttam,* each of 100 verses. In the former work, he mentions an incident in the *Mahābhārata* when Kṛṣṇa hid the sun with his discus to enable Arjuna kill Jayatrata. Though Tirumaḷisai has mentioned many of Kṛṣṇa's childhood exploits,[14] the most interesting reference is to Kṛṣṇa as Gītāchārya[15] and his Visvarūpa form. The Āḷvār says: "People who have not learnt the divine words uttered by the cowherd boy who also revealed his immeasurable proportions (*Visvarūpa*), the king of Dwārakā, are considered as persons without true knowledge."

In his *Tiruchanda-Viruttam,* the Āḷvār gives a detailed account of Kṛṣṇa's early childhood, his slaying of many demons, his subjugation of bulls to marry Pinnai, his role in the Bhārata war. A rare and interesting reference found in his work is to the hunch-backed woman called Naikavakkirai who gave sandal paste to Kṛṣṇa and Balarāma and was cured of her deformity by Kṛṣṇa's grace.[16]

48. Kāliyanardhana, Thanjavur Dt.

50. Kṛṣṇa on the Nāga, Tiruppullani.

51. Kṛṣṇa on the Nāga, Tiruppullani.

49. Nāga stone with Kṛṣṇa, Sevilimedu (near Kānchi).

52. Vēṇugōpāla, Sārangapāni Temple, Kumbakonam.

53. Vēṇugōpāla, National Museum, New Delhi.

55. Chaturbhuja Vēṇugōpāla, Tiruppullani.

54. Vēṇugōpāla, Nāgapattinam (Chennai Museum).

56. Chaturbhuja Vēṇugōpāla, Srirangam.

57. Chaturbhuja Vēṇugōpāla, Tirukkōvalūr.

58. Vēṇugōpāla, Tiruvidandai.

59. Vēṇugōpāla, Vellore.

60. Vēṇugōpāla, Padaividu.

65. Madanagōpāla, Tenkasi.

63. Vēṇugōpāla with Gōpikās, Tirukkodikaval.

61. Vēṇugōpāla (Bronze), Chennai Museum.

62. Vēṇugōpāla (Chola), Tiruvendipuram.

64. Vēṇugōpāla, Srivilliputtur.

Nammāḻvār

Kāri Māran, later honoured by the names Nammāḻvār and Saṭagōpa, was born in a Vellala caste at Kurugur (Āḻvār Tirunagari) near Tirunelveli. He lived during the 8th century A.D. He is regarded as the central figure among the galaxy of the Āḻvārs. His four works namely *Tiruviruttam, Tiruvāsiriyam, Periya-Tiruvantāti* and *Tiruvāymoḻi* are highly valued and revered as the four Tamil Vēdas by the Tamil Vaiṣṇavites. His works give a detailed account of his Kṛṣṇa experience. The fact that the Āḻvār was fascinated by Kṛṣṇavatāra is evident almost in each and every verse. We shall take up the *Tiruvāymoḻi* and study the elaborate treatment of Kṛṣṇavatāra.

The life-story of Kṛṣṇa right from his birth in Mathura,[17] his growth in Gōkula and his destruction of many demons and Kamsa[18] till he became the hero of the Bhārata war,[19] all these episodes are repeatedly alluded to by Nammāḻvār.

Nammāḻvār is often struck with wonder whenever he thinks about the compassion and simplicity of the Lord who took birth as a humble cowherd boy and underwent many punishments like the ordinary mortals. He was tied and beaten for stealing butter. When the popular verse "*patrudai adiyavark-keḻiyavan*" was sung by him, the Āḻvār fell into a trance, as he was overwhelmed by the thought of Kṛṣṇa's easy accessibility.[20]

Once Kṛṣṇa questioned the traditional offerings made to Indra by the cowherds and asked them to worship mount Gōvardhana instead. He took the form of a ghost (Bhūta) and ate everything offered to Indra. When Indra, in great anger, created storm and rains, Kṛṣṇa held up the Mount Gōvardhana like an umbrella and protected the cattle and human beings. The Gōvardhana episode is often mentioned by Nammāḻvār to show the superiority of Kṛṣṇa over other gods.[21]

Kṛṣṇa as a dancer is very popular with the Āḻvārs and is often referred to by them. Nammāḻvar too refers to Kṛṣṇa *Kūttan* (dancer).[22] The most popular dance forms attributed to Kṛṣṇa are *kuravai* and *kuḍam* besides the forms *kāliya-mardana* and *Navanīta-mardana. Kuravai* was like the *rāsa-krīḍā* but not identical.[23] The pot dance (*kuḍakkūttu*) of Kṛṣṇa is frequently mentioned by the Āḻvār.[24]

The theme of Kṛṣṇa subjugating the seven bulls and marrying Nappinnai was a favourite one with the Tamil poets right from the Sangam age. It is more so with the Āḻvārs. Nammāḻvār often speaks about this tradition and treats Pinnai as a consort of Kṛṣṇa, on par with Srīdēvi and Bhūdēvi.[25]

According to Nammāḻvār, the sole purpose of Kṛṣṇavatāra was to protect the good people from the evil forces like Kamsa.[26] After the completion of his mission, Kṛṣṇa (with his kith and kin) went to Saurashtra and established a kingdom with Dwārakā as the capital and himself as the king.[27]

The marriage of Rukmini, daughter of the king of Vidarbha, was fixed with Sisupāla, much against her will. Rukmini wanted to marry none other than Kṛṣṇa and hence sent a message requesting him to come and rescue her. Kṛṣṇa abducted her, defeated her brother and married her.[28]

The story of Uṣa, daughter of Bāṇāsura, and Aniruddha, grandson of Kṛṣṇa, and the subsequent event of war between Kṛṣṇa and Bāṇāsura have been treated by Nammāḷvār elaborately.[29]

When the eldest of the Pāṇḍavas, Yudhistra, performed the *rājasuya-yāga*, it was decided by Bhīṣma that the *agra-pūjā* should be given to Kṛṣṇa and no one else. Sisupāla was against this and openly criticised and humiliated Kṛṣṇa. Kṛṣṇa killed Sisupāla with his discus. The Sisupāla-vadha is mentioned by the Āḷvār.[30]

The war between the Pāṇḍavas and the Kauravas was almost inevitable. Kṛṣṇa, who stood by the Pāṇḍavas, as a last resort to avert the war, went as their messenger to Duryodhana.[31] Kṛṣṇa's humble role as a 'messenger-boy' is highlighted by the Āḷvār. Kṛṣṇa as 'Pāṇḍava-thūtan' is a fine example for his humility and concern for his friends and devotees.

Another humble role that he took as a true friend of the Pāṇḍavas, was to serve as the charioteer to Arjuna, in the great war of Bhārata.[32] Kṛṣṇa as Pārthasārathi had a special appeal to the Āḷvār.[33] He says Kṛṣṇa went as a charioteer in support of five persons (Pāṇḍavas) against a hundred (Kauravas) and crushed the enemies.[34] Kṛṣṇa was the brain behind the Bhārata war. Nammāḷvār describes the Bhārata war as *māyappōr*[35] (a war of wonder).

A rather obscure episode mentioned in the Purāṇas is alluded to by Nammāḷvār. Once a Brahmin came to Arjuna requesting him to save his children who disappeared as soon as they were born. Arjuna in turn sought the help of Kṛṣṇa and both went in search of the children and brought them back from Vaikunta.[36] This is mentioned in the *Bhāgavata Purāṇa* also.

Nammāḷvār assumes the role of a lovelorn lady (*nāyaki*) who thinks of no one but the Lord (*nāyaka*) and who longs to be united with him and has sung songs as a friend and the mother of the girl. A sooth-sayer was invited to examine her and she diagnosed the disease of the girl. The diagnosis of the sooth-sayer forms a decad.[37] Parānkusa-nāyaki, as Nammāḷvār was called in his nāyaki-bhāva, had waited long enough for the arrival of Kṛṣṇa.[38] But he never turned up. Parānkusa-nāyaki decided to perform self-immolation (*maḍal*) though according to the social norms, a woman was prohibited to perform the *maḍal.* In her agony and anguish, she decided to take this extreme step to obtain the grace of the Lord.[39]

Nammāḷvār's Kṛṣṇa-Tṛṣṇa-Tatva

Nammāḷvār suffered from insatiable thirst (*tṛṣṇa*) for Lord Kṛṣṇa. This epithet *Kṛṣṇa-tṛṣṇa* was coined by Parāsara Bhaṭṭa to describe Nammāḷvar's longing for Kṛṣṇa. The traditional belief was that Nammāḷvār lived very close to the time of Kṛṣṇa and he missed him by only a week and hence his special attachment to Kṛṣṇa. Nammāḷvār's Kṛṣṇa-tṛṣṇa is best explained in his own words. He says that Kṛṣṇa was everything to him, the food he ate, the water he drank and the betel leaves he chewed.[39a] Nammāḷvār's profound Kṛṣṇa consciousness finds its echo in the temple of Nammāḷvār at his birth-place Āḷvār Tirunagari. The shrine is studded with Kṛṣṇa sculptures everywhere. Another interesting feature to be noted in the temple is that during the Brahmotsava of Nammāḷvār. On the 9th day, the Āḷvār assumes to be Kṛṣṇa himself and he is taken out in procession as a baby Kṛṣṇa with a butter pot. It is known as '*Vennai Thāzi Thirukkōlam*' in Tamil.

Periyāḷvār

Viṣṇuchitta, known later as Periyāḷvār (the great saint), was a Brahmin from Srivilliputtur. He was supplying garlands every day to the temple as a service. His poems are collectively called *Periyāḷvār Tirumoḷi*. His love for Kṛṣṇa was that of a mother to her child (*mātru-vātsalya*). Of all the aspects of Kṛṣṇa, Periyāḷvār was fascinated by the child Kṛṣṇa. He was so much enthralled by Kṛṣṇa's delightful activities in Gōkulam that he imagined his town as Āyarpadi, himself as Yasōdā, the mother of the divine child, and pours out his heart into his verses. Periyāḷvār is considered to be a pioneer in *piḷḷai-tamil*, a new form of Tamil poetry which he employed to express his innermost yearning for the child Kṛṣṇa. What better way could there be for a poet to bring forth sentiments than to take the role of the mother? His verses constitute a scintillating collection of moving poetry which could be sung by the young and the old alike. In his poems, we get the whole gamut of the life-story of Kṛṣṇa.

The *piḷḷai-tamil* starts with the lullaby or *talāṭṭu* in Tamil. The poet sings songs to make the divine child sleep. This common practice of any mother is beautifully applied to Kṛṣṇa by the Āḷvār. He gives a list of gift articles presented by Brahmā, Siva, Indra, Varuṇa and others to the child Kṛṣṇa.[40]

Inviting the Moon (ambuli paruvam) This practice of showing the moon (*ambuli*) to the child while feeding is common in Indian households. Periyāḷvār invites the moon to come and play with Kṛṣṇa. Many enchanting episodes of Kṛṣṇa are referred to in these verses.[41]

Rhythmic Dance (chengīrai paruvam)[42] One of the games of the early childhood. Yasōdā makes the child Kṛṣṇa move his head and arms rhythmically.

Clapping of Hands (chappāṇi-koṭṭuthal) The child is taught to clap his hands.[43]

Walking (taḷar-naḍai nadattal) The child learns to walk. The mother's joy in seeing her child attempting to walk is boundless and the sentiment is reflected in Periyāḷvār's poems.[44] He experiences the joys of Yasōdā.

Embracing the Mother (achō-paruvam) Yasōdā asks the child Kṛṣṇa to come and embrace her.[45]

Pointing to Objects (appoocchi kāṭṭuthal)[46] In this stage, the child learns to point to objects by using its hands. Here Kṛṣṇa shows the *sankha* and *chakra* with his hands.

Breast Feeding (mulaiyunna azaithal)[47] The Āḷvār having assumed the role of Yasōdā asks Kṛṣṇa to come and be breast fed. This shows to what extent the Āḷvār had involved himself in Kṛṣṇānubhava.

Ear-boring Ceremony (kādu-kuttal)[48] Ear-boring ceremony is common even today in South India. Generally, the child's earlobes are pierced on the first birthday. The poet addresses Kṛṣṇa by twelve names (*Dwādasa-nāmā*) of Viṣṇu. In this decad many customs of the shepherds (āyars) such as *Kuravai* dance are mentioned.

Apart from all the above childhood episodes Periyāḷvār derived pleasure in doing the daily chores for child Kṛṣṇa.

1. *Nīraṭṭal*[49] Periyāḷvār begs Kṛṣṇa to come and take oil-bath (anointment and lustration).
2. *Kuzal vāral*[50] Calling Kṛṣṇa to come and have his hair combed and done into coiffure.
3. *Kōl-konḍu-vā* Addressing the crow to bring a stick for the child to play with.
4. *Pūcchūdal*[51] Flower decoration on the dressed up coiffure.
5. *Kāppidal*[52] Having dressed Kṛṣṇa beautifully, his mother wants to avoid the evil eye (*Kannēru* in Tamil) by performing *ārti.* It is still being done in temples and households.

Periyāḷvār, having experienced the joys of bringing up the child Kṛṣṇa, also realises the difficulty in controlling the pranks of the naughty boy in his boyhood and adolescent age. The Āḷvār gives a detailed account of his mischievous acts such as snatching the clothes and bangles of the girls who were bathing in the Yamunā,[53] stealing butter,[54] putting live ants into the ears of calves,[55] teasing the young cowherd girls by destroying their small sand houses in their simulated play (*citril*)[56] and many more. On hearing the complaints of the gōpikās, the Āḷvār, as Kṛṣṇa's mother, scolds the child.[57]

So far, Periyāḷvār's maternal sentiments dominated his verses. In other hymns, he describes the feelings of the young ladies towards Kṛṣṇa. They are attracted by his lovely face, and are waiting in the streets just to see his smiling face, his dancing form, his beautiful body and to hear his melodious flute.[58] The impact of Kṛṣṇa's flute on the living and non-living creatures is enchantingly described by the Āḷvār in a decad.[59] Hearing the sweet music of his flute, the girls of the cowherd colony (*iḍaichēri*) came out running, leaving their homes, relatives and their belongings.

One such girl's mother worries about her daughter who has fallen in love with Kṛṣṇa. She is so obsessed with him that she is even prepared to leave her home to be with him. In such love poems three characters are important: *nāyaki* (heroine) as the love-sick girl, her mother and her friend. The poet plays all the three roles and gives a dramatic touch to the poetry. This was popular in the *Ahapporuḷ* literature of the Sangam period. Here, Periyāḷvār plays all the three roles but the hymns of the mother are the most touching as they symbolically show his own feelings on his only daughter Āṇḍāḷ's love for Kṛṣṇa and her ultimate union with the Lord.[60]

Periyāḷvār has also dedicated his poems to temples like Tirumālirunchōlai, Tirukkottiyur, Srirangam and Tirupati. He describes the hill of Tirumālirunchōlai as the abode of Kṛṣṇa.[61]

Periyāḷvār begins the decad on Tiruvarangam with two puranic stories according to which Kṛṣṇa restored to life the son of his Guru Santipini and the children of a Brahmin.[62] The Āḷvār's thorough knowledge of puranic lores is evident in his description of even obscure events.

Periyāḷvār was not only familiar with the Sangam tradition but also continued it which is evident from his description of Kṛṣṇa's *kuḍam* dance[63] and his subjugation of seven bulls to marry Nappinnai.[64] *Kuḍam* dance was one of the sixteen dances mentioned in ancient Tamil works. In this form of dance the performer held many pots on the head and shoulders, while dancing he would joggle with the pots in his hands. *Kuḍa-kūttu* as it is called in Tamil is a dance form peculiar to Kṛṣṇa.[65]

In another set of ten beautiful verses Peryāḷvār brings out the comparison and contrast between Rāmāvatāra and Kṛṣṇavatāra.[66] It is a kind of song sung for a folk dance of Tamilnāḍu known as *Undipara.* We learn from the epic *Silappadikāram* that the *Undipara* was one of the many ancient dance forms like the *Kolāṭṭam* or *Kummi* danced by young girls, singing the stories of Kṛṣṇa or Rāma.

In the decad about Kṛṣṇa's *taḷar-naḍai* (learning to walk) the Āḷvār describes that the tiny feet of Kṛṣṇa have the marks of *sankha* and *chakra* and when he walks he leaves the marks on the floor.[67] It is interesting to note that even now, on the birthday of Kṛṣṇa (Gokulāshṭami), womenfolk paint his feet from the entrance gate to the interior of the house to denote Kṛṣṇa's arrival to their homes.

A very interesting anecdote not mentioned in the Purāṇas is narrated by Periyāḻvār.[68] It goes as follows: Simāli who pretended to be a friend of Kṛṣṇa learnt the secrets of weaponry from him except that of the discus (*chakra*). Kṛṣṇa came to know about his wicked intentions and wanted to put an end to him. One day, Simāli asked Kṛṣṇa to teach him the use of the *chakra*. Kṛṣṇa told him that it was not easy like other weapons. But Simāli insisted. Kṛṣṇa took the *chakra* in his finger, threw it up in the air and had it back in his hand. Simāli also tried likewise. But when the *chakra* came down, it took his head away.

Āṇḍāḷ

In the works of Āṇḍāḷ (also known as Kōdai or Gōda), Periyāḻvār's adopted daughter, we see a different kind of sentiment expressed i.e. that of a love-lorn maiden for union with her beloved (*nāyaka nāyaki-bhāva*). It is described as bridal mysticism. Assuming herself as a *gōpikā*, Āṇḍāḷ pours out her passionate love and longing for Kṛṣṇa in her poems which are charged with her intense *Kṛṣṇa-prēma*.

Āṇḍāḷ, brought up by Periyāḻvār, himself a great devotee of Kṛṣṇa, was naturally drawn towards Kṛṣṇa, and expressed her wish to marry him and none else. For attaining such a state one must raise oneself above the level of ordinary human beings by performing austerities (*vratas* or *nōnbu*) through sincere devotion (*bhakti*) and complete surrender (*prapatti*). One such austerity is known as *pāvai-nōnbu* in Tamil. Her popular work *Tiruppāvai* is about this *nōnbu* performed by Āṇḍāḷ to have the Lord's grace to do eternal service to him.

Where was she going to perform the *nōnbu*? According to the *Viṣṇu Purāṇa*,[69] once when Kṛṣṇa was performing the Rāsa-dance with the *gōpikās*, he suddenly disappeared, leaving the girls alone. The *gōpis* enticed by the beauty and love of Kṛṣṇa were not able to bear the separation of their lord and started enacting Kṛṣṇa's childhood sports. One girl, assuming herself as Kṛṣṇa, enacted the Kāḷiyamardana scene; another pretended as if she were killing Dhēnuka. By these actions, they had a feeling that they were constantly in the company of Kṛṣṇa, though in reality he was not with them. Āṇḍāḷ by her poetic excellence and imagination brought the whole atmosphere of Gōkula to her native place Srivilliputtūr. She assumed Srivilliputtūr as Tiruvāypāḍi (Gōkulam), the womenfolk of the place as cowherd girls, and herself as a *gōpi*. She also assumed Vaḍaperunkōil to be Nandagopa's palace, the deity of the temple as Kṛṣṇa and performed the *nōnbu*. This is a classic example of the process of localisation of myths that acted as an important means to spread of puranic episodes and preserve the tradition in different parts of India.

Besides attaining a good husband the reason for performing the austerity was to have regular rains, to have a good harvest, to get more milk from the cows for the welfare of the community.[70] The purpose of the *nōnbu* was to secure the blessings of Lord Kṛṣṇa and to be at his service for ever.[71] The details of the austerities to be observed to attain the Lord are portrayed in this beautiful poem *Tiruppāvai.*

In another long poem of 143 verses entitled *Nācchiyār Tirumoḷi*, Āṇḍāḷ describes her mystical marriage with Kṛṣṇa.

Āṇḍāḷ worships *Kāma* (Indian cupid), the God of love, to secure his help to have the union with Kṛṣṇa.[72] The festival of Kāma (*tai-nirāḍal*) was well known in Tamilnāḍu even in the Sangam age. The young and unmarried girls used to worship Kāma to get a good husband. Āṇḍāḷ's poems give a detailed and sequential account of the Kāma-Pūjā.

Firstly, during the months of *Thai-Māsi* (January-February), she cleaned and decorated the streets by which Kāma was coming, and prepared the stage. She painted the name of Kāma on the wall along with his flags, horses, maidens and also the sugarcane bow and offered beautiful and fragrant flowers to Kāma and worshipped him. She prayed to him to unite her with the Lord of Dwārakā (*Tuvara*).[73]

In the following month, *Panguni*, Āṇḍāḷ celebrated a *nōnbu* to get the blessings of Kāma. She offered paddy, sugarcane, jaggery and rice to Kāma and arranged for the recitation of the *mantras* by the Brahmins. She ate only once a day and worshipped Kāma three times a day during the *nōnbu.* She says "I did all these things to be at the service of Kṛṣṇa and Kāmadēva must help me to have the honour of touching the feet of the Lord."[74]

Āṇḍāḷ, in a set of ten verses entitled *Kūḍal Iḷaithal*, refers to an ancient method to find out whether one's wishes would come true or not. One should draw a big circle on sand and inside it many concentric circles should be drawn with one's eyes closed. On counting the number of circles if it was an even number then the answer was in the affirmative and if it was an odd number it was negative. Āṇḍāḷ wants to find out whether she would be united with the Lord. She prays for getting an even number to succeed in her venture.

Āṇḍāḷ describes to her friend the sweet dream she had in which she married Kṛṣṇa. The ten verses give a vivid description of a South Indian wedding.[75] The first verse says the Lord as the bridegroom is coming surrounded by thousand elephants and celestials including Indra and people welcome him with *pūrṇakalasa* an auspicious symbol. After the grand reception, the groom is seated on a decorated dais.

Āṇḍāḷ the bride is dressed with a special wedding saree (*kōti*) by Durgā.[76] Āṇḍāḷ is also garlanded by Durgā who is a sister of Kṛṣṇa. In South India, the sister of the groom plays an important role in her brother's wedding. She is the one who helps the bride to wear *kōti* even now. Then Āṇḍāḷ describes the ritual of tying the small yellow threads on the arms of both the bride and the groom. It is called *kankaṇ*. Then in the midst of auspicious music and the sound of drums and conches Kṛṣṇa holds the hand of Āṇḍāḷ and the couple go round the Agni (fire) to sanctify their relationship.

Another important ritual follows: The Lord with his beautiful arm picks up the foot of Āṇḍāḷ and places it on a stone-mortar. This is known as *ammi-midthithal* without which the marriage is incomplete even today. These ten verses of Āṇḍāḷ describing her dream marriage with Kṛṣṇa have become so famous that they are recited regularly in the marriages in Vaiṣṇava houses of Tamilnāḍu even today.

Āṇḍāḷ, following her father, dedicated her hymns to temples like *Tiruvēngadam, Tirumālirunsōlai* and *Tiruvarangam.* She attributes many childhood feats of Kṛṣṇa to the presiding deities of these temples. She sends the clouds, the Koyal bird and the conch as her messengers to Lord Kṛṣṇa and requests him to come and save her life.

Āṇḍāḷ, unable to bear the separation any more, pleads with her people to take her to Mathura, or to Gōkula, or to the banks of the river Yamunā, or to Dwārakā or some other place connected with Kṛṣṇa to have his *darshan,* for he alone can save her (*TNB,* 12).

The last set of ten verses are said to have been sung after Āṇḍāḷ had the delightful vision of Lord Kṛṣṇa (*Brindāvanathē Kaṇḍomē*).

Kulasēkarāḷvār

Kulasēkara, the Chera king who turned a saint, was a leading light of the Bhakti movement and has written 105 verses, collectively known as *Perumāl-Tirumoḷi.* It is well known that he was a great devotee of Rāma. That did not prevent him from composing two beautiful decads on Kṛṣṇa exclusively.

The 6th decad of his work was composed as a series of complaints of the gōpikās to Yasōdā. They blame Kṛṣṇa for his infidelity towards them and his bundle of lies and deceitful activities. One girl asks him how he could misbehave with her servant-maid.[77] Another girl swears that she would not be carried away by his sugar-coated lies any more.[78]

Kulasēkara's verses contain some unusual and soulful experiences. Of the two mothers of Kṛṣṇa, Dēvaki who gave birth to Kṛṣṇa and Yasōdā the foster mother, the latter was more fortunate as she could enjoy the pleasure of bringing up the divine child and witnessing all the super-human acts of the child. Whereas Periyāḷvār took the role of the foster mother and described her joyful experiences with the different stages of child's life, Kulasēkara's sympathies turn towards the less fortunate mother, Dēvaki. The Āḷvār places himself in her position and gives expression to her sorrow of not being able to bring up her own child. Dēvaki was cruelly deprived of the joy of bringing up her child. According to the Āḷvār, when Kṛṣṇa after killing Kamsa returned to Mathura to fulfil his mission, he met his parents for the first time. The real mother Dēvaki poured out her pent-up feelings to her son. The Āḷvār used this dramatic situation and composed one decad on Dēvaki's inner longing for her son.

Dēvaki laments that she did not have the pleasure of listening to the lisping words of her child Kṛṣṇa nor feeding him nor witnessing several of his mischievous but delightful pranks like stealing butter and getting caught and pretending to apologise and weep.[79]

Dēvaki tells Kṛṣṇa, "I was not fortunate enough to see any of your sports such as holding up the Gōvardhana hill as an umbrella, Kuravai and Kuḍam dance, killing of demons, and the Kāḷiyamardana." She tells him if he could make her see all these feats in any way, she would be grateful indeed.[80]

Toṇḍaraḍipoḍi Āḷvār

Vipranārāyaṇa, also known as Toṇḍar-aḍi-poḍi (meaning "the dust of the feet of a devotee"), has two works *Tirumālai* and *Tirupalli-eḷucchi* to his credit. Both the works are in praise of the Lord of Srirangam. He vehemently condemns the caste and class distinctions and extolls the virtues of pure and simple devotion and selfless service to the Lord and his devotees. Toṇḍaraḍipoḍi Āḷvār spent his life as a garland-maker to the Lord of Srirangam, who was none other than Kṛṣṇa himself. He says, Kṛṣṇa has captured his heart and soul.

Tirupānāḷvār

He belonged to the low caste of street singers, known as Pānars in Tamil. The *Guruparamparai* says that Lord Ranganātha, pleased with his devotion, asked the head priest of the temple to carry Pānar on his shoulders to the temple, when the latter was prohibited to enter the temple of Srirangam. This is a clear indication of how the people of the high castes were forced to recognise the true devotees irrespective of their caste, creed or sex. In his work *Amalanādipirān,* he pours out his heart to Kṛṣṇa. He says that Kṛṣṇa stole not only the butter but also the hearts of his devotees.

Tirumangai Āḻvār

Kaliyan, born in Kurayalūr near Tirunagari in Sirgali taluk in Tanjore district, was a chieftain of Āli Nāḍu under the Pallavas. He was a contemporary of Nandivarman Pallavamalla (731-796 A.D.). Later he came to be known as Tirumangai Āḻvār and it is said he spent all his wealth to feed the Bhāgavatas or the devotees of Viṣṇu and to construct temples for the Lord.[81]

Tirumangai's poems are classified under six sections, namely, "*Periya Tirumoḻi*", "*Tiruneḍunthāṇḍakam*", "*Tirukuruthāṇḍakam*", "*Tiruvelukkutirukkai*", "*Siriya Tirumaḍal*" and "*Periya Tirumaḍal*" in the *Nālāyira-Divya Prabandham,* thus forming the second major contribution, next only to Nammāḻvār. Just as the works of Nammāḻvār are regarded as the Four Vedas in Tamil, the works of Tirumangai are regarded as the Six Vedāngas in Tamil by the Vaiṣṇavas of Tamilnāḍu.

We get very detailed and repeated descriptions of Kṛṣṇa stories, running through the entire gamut of his works. Among the Āḻvārs, it was Tirumangai who was sung about in the largest number of shrines, not only in South, but also in North India. We can review a few selected instances and special literary forms, to illustrate his deep and abiding devotion to Kṛṣṇa.

Many Kṛṣṇa temples near his place of birth attracted the Āḻvār. He visited them and glorified them in his hymns. They are: *Kāvalambāḍi, Pārthan Paḷḷi, Arimeya Viṇṇagaram* in Tirunāngūr, *Therazundūr* and *Chidambaram.* We shall deal with them briefly.

Kāvalambāḍi[82] The name of the place itself denotes the Lord (Kṛṣṇa) who killed the elephant. Many exploits of Kṛṣṇa such as defeating Indra to get the *Karpaga* tree for Satyabhāmā and killing the elephant Kuvalayāpita are all glorified in his verses, dedicated to this temple.

Pārthan Paḷḷi Here the Āḻvār takes the role of the mother and sings hymns on the Lord of Pārthan Paḷḷi, another form of Kṛṣṇa.

Arimēya Viṇṇagar Not far from his birth-place, another Kṛṣṇa temple which evoked Tirumangai's praise is Arimēya Viṇṇagar. He describes the Lord appropriately as *Kudamādum Kuttan*[83] (one who danced with the pots). The chief idol of the *mūla vigraha* of this temple where Kṛṣṇa is seated with one foot on the pot exactly fits in with his description.

Tiruvalundūr or Thērazundūr[84] In the decad dedicated to this place where the presiding deity is Kṛṣṇa in the form of a cowherd boy as the name

Āmaruviyappan indicates, the Āḷvār, as the *nāyaki*, expresses her love and affection for her beloved.

Tiruchitrakūḍam (Chidambaram) Here is the famous temple of Naṭarāja and within its complex is the shrine for Viṣṇu as Gōvindarāja. The processional deity is Pārthasārathi who is glorified in the hymns of Tirumangai Āḷvār.

Besides these, many other Kṛṣṇa temples such as *Tiruvallikeni* (in Chennai city), an ancient and well-known shrine for Pārthasārathi, are celebrated ones: *Tirukkovalur, Tirukannapuram, Tirukannamangai, Kannan Kabisthalam, Tirukannankudi*—these five form the Pancha Kṛṣṇa Kshētras. All these have been sung by Tirumangai. In all these songs marked by rich poetry the Āḷvār derives his inspiration from the playful sports of Lord Kṛṣṇa.

The Āḷvār was so possessed with the Kṛṣṇa consciousness that even when he was singing about Srirangam,[85] he attributes Kṛṣṇa stories to the Lord Ranganātha. Even obscure incidents (such as rescuing the sons of a Brahmin) from the Purāṇas have found expression in his poems.[86]

The greatness of Kṛṣṇavatāra is mentioned in a verse which describes the aspect of Nara and Nārāyaṇa and his exposition of the *Gītā*.[87] In the same verse the Āḷvār describes Kṛṣṇa's Visvarūpa form.

Tirumangai Āḷvār has also sung twenty songs in *Piḷḷai-tamil* form in praise of Kṛṣṇa, like Periyāḷvār, though not so elaborately. One or two stages of the child's growth have been described.[88] He repeatedly reminds us of the twin aspects of the Lord—the supreme *Paratva* and the *Saulabhya*, the easy accessibility to his devotees. This is the central idea of the Bhāgavata philosophy.[89]

Maḍal The most important and noteworthy poems of Tirumangai Āḷvār, as far as our topic is concerned, are the *Periya-tirumaḍal* and *Siriya-tirumaḍal* which are considered as two single poems. *Maḍal* or *Maḍalūral* is an old Tamil custom which was practised by the rejected lover to win the heart of his beloved. It seems that the love-sick young man without taking bath, food, drink and even without sleep, would wander in streets, talking and singing about his beloved. At last, when these things fail to win the heart of his girl, he would try to commit suicide, right in front of his love. In most cases, it would end up in happy union as the girls are invariably moved by the sincere affection and love. We get plenty of references to this custom in the Sangam works. It must have been a common practice among men in those days. Women were prohibited to perform *maḍal* under any circumstance. The ancient Tamil work *Tirukkuraḷ* says: "Even if their love (*Kāma*) is as large as an Ocean, women will not resort to *maḍalūrthal*.[90]

Tirumangai Āḷvār assumes the role of a *gōpikā*, languishing in love for Kṛṣṇa and decides to perform *maḍalūrthal*. How can the Āḷvār as a girl practise this? The Āḷvār himself answers this question. "We have heard that woman must not practise *maḍal* to get her lover according to Tamil tradition, but I shall not accept this and I shall follow the northern (Sanskrit) literary tradition (which permits womenfolk to perform *maḍal*)."

In the *Siriya-tirumaḍal*, the Āḷvār assumes the role of a maiden (nāyaki) and describes her romantic encounter with Kṛṣṇa. She says: "One day when I was playing with my friends, a girl came and invited us to come and witness the pot-dance performed by a young man whose name was Māl (Viṣṇu). It was my bad time that I went there and the result was, I lost my complexion, my bangles and even my mind in the bargain."

The girl's mother was shocked to see her daughter in such a pitiable state. On the advice of the elders, she consulted a lady soothsayer (*Kuratti*) to find out the real cause of her ailment. The latter examined her and said that she was possessed of a divine power and that a black-complexioned person wearing *tulasi* (basil leaf) garland and holding the *sankha* and *chakra* had taken possession of her heart. She also added that he was none other than the Lord who had measured the universe, who lifted the Govardhana hill, who grazed the cattle etc. From the description, the mother understood that it was Kṛṣṇa. The girl confesses and explains: "What am I to do? There is no one who can help me. How can I forget Kṛṣṇa when my mouth repeatedly utters his name?" She decides to perform the *Maḍalūrthal* and go about visiting all his sacred shrines praying for his mercy and grace, not minding the criticism of the public. She also justifies her action by citing the example of Vāsavadattai of the puranic fame who went with her lover, leaving all her relatives.

Tirumangai Āḷvār's other work *Periya-tirumaḍal* is also written on the same model with the same sentiments. Thus the *maḍal* form, which was common in the *Ahapporul* and secular literature of the Sangam age, was handled by the Āḷvārs to show their religious sentiments.

The puranic stories in Sanskrit were narrated by the Āḷvārs in Tamil for the benefit of the common man. Though the percolation of the puranic lore can be traced to some extent even in the Sangam literature, its development in full-fledged form with emotional and devotional attachment is to be seen in the works of the Āḷvārs. The poems of the Āḷvārs dealt with them more elaborately and their treatment was with the purpose of highlighting the greatness of Viṣṇu through his various incarnations, particularly Kṛṣṇa and to popularise Bhāgavatism.

Impact of Bhakti Movement

The liberal religious trends set in motion in the Bhakti period brought about some significant developments in the social and religious contexts.

The earlier mode of worship with its emphasis on the Vēdic rituals and sacrifices was relegated to the background. In its place came the new Bhakti religion. The Āḷvārs did not discard the Vēdas and gave them their due regard, but modified their import. They disowned the caste distinctions prevalent in the society. They felt that sincere love, devotion and service to God was more important than the status of the worshipper, and the quantity of the offerings. They went even a step further and said that the complete surrender to the God's will was the only way to salvation, and that could be attained only by *Tonḍu* (*Kainkarya* in Sanskrit) or service to the idol consecrated in the temples. The icon has become the very life-breath of the temple worship. The Āḷvārs considered the idol as an incarnation of Viṣṇu in the Kāli Age and a new word *archāvatāra* was coined by the later Vaiṣṇavites to signify this idea.

As a result, the temple and the icon in it became more and more important. The Āḷvārs were drawn to the holy places of India like Badrinath, Mathura, Brindāvan, Dwārakā, Ayōdhya and Neimisāranya which were associated with Kṛṣṇa and Rāma. They visited numerous holy places in Tamilnāḍu and sang in praise of the Lord. They dedicated their hymns to the temples they visited and brought them nearer to the hearts and minds of Tamil people by their beautiful hymns in Tamil.

The Tamil term *tonḍu* (bodily service) is broad in the sense that it consists of many devotional activities such as worshipping the idols, visiting temples, seeing the Lord, praising and saluting not only the Lord but also his true devotees (*aḍiyārs* or Bhāgavatas). It also includes cleaning the temple, anointing and decorating the idol and making offerings, ablutions and gifts. The Āḷvārs accepted *tonḍu* or service to God and His devotees as total way of life which demanded selfless dedication to the Lord in all their actions. In Periyāḷvār's words he and his family members were marked by the temple seal to be the willing slaves of the Lord.[91] Periyāḷvār and Tondaradipodiāḷvār were supplying garlands regularly to the temples of Srivilliputtūr and Srirangam respectively. Tirumangaiāḷvār is said to have fed the Bhāgavatas daily and built the compound wall of the Srirangam temple. Thus, for them, visiting temples, singing hymns in praise of the Lord, doing bodily services and serving the devotees of the Lord were the noblest forms of Bhakti as against asceticism. In the fraternity of the Bhāgavatas (*Tondar-kula*) there was no place for caste-distinctions.

Purāṇic stories were often narrated by the Āḷvārs to glorify the Lord's abundant grace, mercy and readiness to protect his devotees. They also connected the myths with the local temples. They sought to establish a link between the idol and the ancient Purāṇic myths. It might have also served as a reconciliation between the Vēdic and Purāṇic ideas and the Bhāgavata movement. In order to elevate the status of the temple worship and to sanctify the idol worship, against the Vēdic orthodoxy, the Āḷvārs must have thought that the association of the temples and the deities with the Purāṇas or Epics was necessary. The result was the development of the process of localisation of the puranic episodes in their poems.

Many new literary forms came up in Tamil during this period, besides the continuation of the old literary forms. The tenet of dedicating poems to temples is new to Tamil language, introduced by the Āḷvārs. *Pillaitamil* form for the first time is introduced by Periyāḷvār. We have already seen its nature, earlier in this chapter. It was used for religious purpose with a god or a goddess as its central figure. Later on, it came to be used for secular purposes having popular personalities as the hero.

On the other hand, many literary forms which were secular in nature in the Sangam *Ahapporuḷ* tradition were now applied for expressing religious as well as spiritual sentiments by the Āḷvārs. The most important of these are the *maḍal* and the *nāyaki-bhāva.* Āḷvārs like Nammāḷvār, Tirumangai and Āṇḍāḷ have poured forth many poems of the above types, assuming the role of the beloved and appealing to the Lord. The under-current philosophy is the longing soul, seeking to be at the feet of the Lord and thus avoid the cycle of re-births.

Royal Efforts

Along with the temple-worship grew the rituals, festivals and the patronage in the form of endowments. The royal patronage to the Vēdic rites and *yagnas* began to decline after the 9th century. During the 7th and 8th centuries A.D. we see some Pallava and Pāṇḍya kings priding themselves with having performed sacrifices such as *Vājapēya* and *Gōsahasra.* This trend did not continue for long. The kings recognised the growing popularity of this movement at the mass level and wanted to take advantage of it by actively associating themselves with the temple movement and extended patronage and support to the new form of temple-centred religion.

Some of the kings like Mahēndravarman I and Ninrasīr Nedumāran who showed some lenience towards Jainism were also brought back into the Brahmanical fold. The Buddhist and Jain influences began to diminish and disappear altogether. As a result, the cults of Vaiṣṇavism and Saivism received the royal patronage and flourished under the aegis of the rulers. There are quite a few complimentary references to the Pāṇḍya and Pallava rulers in the poems of Periyāḷvār and Tirumangaiāḷvār. We also have the supporting evidence in the form of copper plates and inscriptions to show that many of the Pāṇḍya and Pallava rulers called themselves as *Parama Bhāgavatas* and *Parama Māhēsvaras.*

Pāṇḍyas

The Pāṇḍyas of Madurai, as pointed out in the first chapter, followed the tradition of associating themselves with the Pāṇḍavas of *Mahābhārata.* We get many such references even in the Sangam corpus and later on in their copper plates. One of the Pāṇḍya rulers who was a Vaiṣṇava was Varaguṇa I. His minister was known as Māran Kāri or Madhura Kavi. He was a Vaiṣṇava and was responsible for excavating a cave temple for Narasimha in Ānaimalai near Madurai.[92] Some scholars think that he became the disciple of Nammāḻvār and later came to be known as Madhurakavi-āḻvār. The ten verses sung in praise of his guru Nammāḻvār are included in the *Four Thousand* collection. In the very first verse he mentions his deep reverence to Kṛṣṇa.

Varaguṇa Pāṇḍya I (A.D. 770) is referred to as *Parama-vaiṣṇava* in his Srīvaramangala copper plates. He was followed by Srīmāran Srī Vallaban who ruled from A.D. 835 to 885. He was also a Vaiṣṇava. According to the *Guruparampara,*[93] Periyāḻvār established the supremacy of Viṣṇu in the court of Srivallabha and was honoured by the Pāṇḍya king. The king was also known as Kō-Nedumāran and Srīmāran. Periyāḻvār refers to him as a devotee and patron of the temple of Kṛṣṇa at Tirumalirunsōlai. His son Parāntaka Vīranārāyaṇa succeeded him to the throne. He was the author of Dalavāypuram copper plates in which the invocatory verse is dedicated to Viṣṇu.[93a]

Pallavas of Kānchi

The Pallava kings with their capital at Kānchi ruled over the Toṇḍaimaṇḍalam and most of the Chōḻamaṇḍalam for nearly 4 to 5 centuries. Though the Pallava kings generally patronised both Vaiṣṇavism and Saivism without any difference, some of the kings seem to have favoured Saivism and some Vaiṣṇavism. Many kings had names like Viṣṇugōpa, Simha Viṣṇu, Simhavarman and Narasimhavarman. Many of the kings called themselves as *Parama Bhāgavatas.*[94] An inscription of 7th century A.D. contains the eulogy of the king Simhavarman who is stated to have been born in the Pallava family as God Visvaksena (Viṣṇu) was born in the Vṛṣṇi race. They built many temples for Viṣṇu and Kṛṣṇa. Most of their copper plates begin with invocatory verses dedicated to Viṣṇu. The Pallava kings' contribution to Vaiṣṇavism was great and often praised by the Āḻvārs like Tirumangai. From the Tandan Thōṭṭam and Kasakkudi copper plates we know that the king Nandivarman II was a Viṣṇu-bhakta. The copper plate says that a village was given as a grant to 308 well-versed Brahmins and arrangement was made for conducting a discourse on the *Mahābhārata* in the temple premises. Vaikuṇṭa Perumāḷ temple of Kānchi was built by him. It contains many beautiful sculptures of Kṛṣṇa theme.

Chōḷa Kings

The Chōḷa kings were invariably Saivites. However, during their period (c. 850-1250 A.D.) temples for Viṣṇu in general and independent temples for Kṛṣṇa in particular came to be constructed. (This is discussed in detail in Chapter IV.) There are also epigraphical references to the popularity of Kṛṣṇa worship during the Chōḷa period. An inscription ascribable to A.D. 922 from Erode says that the people of a whole *nāḍu* paid some cesses for instituting the worship of Kṛṣṇa in a Viṣṇu temple in the place. The great Chōḷa king Rājarāja I, though an ardent Saivite, arranged for the installation and worship of the image of Vāsudeva in the Great Temple, Thanjavur and a few other places like Tirunelveli.[95] The Chōḷa kings like Kulōttunga I and Vikrama Chōḷa gave tax-free land grants to many Viṣṇu temples such as Srirangam. Their queens also donated gardens and jewels to the temple of Srirangam. Several inscriptions speak about the services done by the Chōḷa ministers to Viṣṇu temples. A general by name Naralōka Vīra donated a fruit garden for Kṛṣṇa shrine at Kānchi.[96] The inscriptional evidences show the continued royal patronage even in the time of the Chōḷas. It further became stronger in the time of the Hoysaḷas and the Vijayanagar kings.

Thus, the newly revived and modified form of Vaiṣṇavism became stronger on one side by the support of royal patronage and on the other side the growing popularity of the Tamil hymns of the Āḻvārs. The devotional lyrics of the Āḻvārs were collected, codified and introduced in the temple service by Nātamuni in 10th century A.D. The Tamil hymns came to be treated with reverence as *Drāvida-Vēda* on par with the Vēdas, and were introduced in the temple rituals, along with the Vēdas. Many grants were given for the recitation of the poems of the Āḻvārs. A Pāṇḍyan inscription mentions the recitation of the hymns of Āṇḍāḷ (*Kōdaipāṭṭu*) before the deity in the temple at Aḻagar Kōil.[97]

Another inscription of Kulōttunga Chōḷa I, dated in 1085 A.D., in Srirangam temple registers the gift of lands by an army commander Āyar Koḷundu Chakrapāṇi for the recitation of *Tiruppāvai* and *Tiruvāymoḻi* in the temple.[98]

The Tamil hymns have in due course become an inseparable part of the temple worship. Whenever the deity is taken out in procession, the Tamil scholars go in front reciting the verses and the Vēdic reciters would follow the deity. The belief is that while the Vēdas go in search of God, the latter goes after the sacred Tamil hymns of His devotees. Besides this, during each temple ritual appropriate hymns are sung. For example, during the bathing ritual (*Tirumañjanam*), Periyāḻvār's *Nīrāḍal* poems are recited. The temple rituals are incomplete without the recitation of the Tamil hymns of the Āḻvārs. They have also been introduced in the marriage rituals and other social functions of the Vaiṣṇava community.[99]

66. Madanagōpāla, Kānchi.

68. Vastrāpaharaṇa scene, Kānchi.

67. Vastrāpaharaṇa scene, Kānchi.

71. Rājamannār, Chennai Museum.

69. Vastrāpaharaṇa scene, Vellore.

70. Vastrāpaharaṇa scene, Tiruvadandai.

74. Rājagōpāla with consorts, Adikudi.

75. Rājagōpāla with consorts, Seramadevi.

76. Rājamannār with consorts, Los Angeles County Museum.

73. Rājamannār, Sundaraperumal Temple, Thanjavur.

78. Rājagōpāla, National Museum, New Delhi.

81. Kṛṣṇa and Rukmini, Kumbakonam.

80. Kṛṣṇa and gōpi, Kānchipuram.

77. Rājamannār, Nilappadai.

79. Holi festival scene, Srīrangam.

82. Gītāchārya, Perambalur.

83. Gītāchārya, Ennaiyiram.

86. Anantakṛṣṇa, Nāgarkōil.

87. Vittaladēva, Kānchipuram.

The later Vaiṣṇava *āchāryas* (Teachers) wrote elaborate commentaries (*Vyākhyānas*) on the poems of the Āḷvārs. They gave regular discourses in the temple premises, thus popularising their ideals and philosophy. The importance of their commentaries for the continuity of Viṣṇu/Kṛṣṇa devotion in Tamilnāḍu is discussed in the next chapter.

Several Sanskrit works were written on the basis of Āḷvārs' Tamil hymns. Many scholars are of the opinion that the *Bhāgavata Purāṇa* was probably written in South India and it shows many influences from the Bhakti movement of the Āḷvārs. They cite internal evidences in the *BGP* which make reference to the people of Drāvida-dēsa for their devotion and to many holy places in South India (F. Hardy).

We also have a post-factum prophecy in the *BGP*[100] stating that many great devotees of Vāsudēva would be born in the Tamil country on the banks of the rivers Kaveri, Tāmaraparṇi, Pālār, Vaigai and Periyār. According to Van Buitenen this awareness of the *BGP* about the appearance of the Tamil saints namely the Āḷvārs and their poems in praise of Lord Kṛṣṇa provides the *terminus post-quem* for the work that it must have been written soon after the Vaiṣṇava movement in South India.[101] Another explanation would be that the references cited above were the later additions to the original *BGP* text.

Above all, the *BGP* stands even today as a testament for the Bhāgavatism and it echoes all the sentiments, emotions, and philosophy of the Tamil saints—Āḷvārs. For the Āḷvārs and the *BGP* the world was the manifestation of Viṣṇu with emphasis on Kṛṣṇa as the most perfect *avatāra* (*pūrṇāvatāra*).

The other works in Sanskrit and *maṇipravāḷa* that owe their inspiration to the Āḷvārs' hymns are discussed in the next chapter.

References

1. *Pāndiar Seppedugal Pattu*, p. 22.
2. Arunachalam, M., *Kalabhras*, 1980.
3. Venkataraman, K.R., *Kalabhras*, *J.I.H.*
4. Tirumangai Āḷvār's hymns on Triplicane refer to the deity as *Vēdattin suvai-payanai*, the quintessence of the Vēdas.
5. These ideas are expounded by Piḷḷai Lōkāchārya in his well-known work *Srī-Vachana Bhūshana* (see Chapter III also).
6. *Tirumālai*, v. 42 and 43.

6a. *Tiruppallāndu*, v. 5.

7. *MTV*, V.39.
8. *MTV*, V.26.
9. *MTV*, V.77.

10. II TV, V.8; 9; V.15; V.19; 62; 63; V.89; V.98.
11. II TV, V.28.
12. III TV, V.16.
13. III TV, V.28.
14. *NTV*, V.33.
15. *NTV*, V.71.
16. *TCV*, V.30.
17. *TVM*, 7-10-4; *TVM*, 8-1-3.
18. *TVM*, 1-5-9; *TVM*, 2-1-8; *TVM*, 4-5-1; *TVM*, 3-5-5.
19. *TVM*, 5-7-4; *TVM*, 6-4-10.
20. *TVM*, 1-3-1: *Ethiramenra aḷavilē mōhittavar ivarē* (Periavachan Pillai).
21. *TVM*, 5-10-5; 1-8-4; *TVM*, 3-3-8.
22. *TVM*, 2-2-11; *TVM*, 4-4-6.
23. *TVM*, 6-4-1.
24. *TVM*, 2-5-11; *TVM*, 2-7-4; *TVM*, 3-6-3:7.
25. *TVM*, 1-5-1; *TVM*, 8-3-1: *Pūmagaḷ manmagaḷ āymagaḷ sanku chakra kai avan...*
26. *TVM*, 3-5-5.
27. *TVM*, 5-3-6.
28. *TVM*, 7-10-6.
29. *TVM*, 2-4-2; 3-8-9; 3-10-4.
30. *TVM*, 7-5-3.
31. *TVM*, 6-6-4: *Nādudai mannarkkut thutu sel nambikku.*
32. *TVM*, 3-6-10: "...*Pandu nūṟṟuvar adavarum padaimadanga Ivarkkāyi venchamattu arru thēr kadaviya perumān*".
33. *TVM*, 7-8-3; 7-5-9.
34. *TVM*, 7-5-9.
35. *TVM*, 5-7-4; 5-10-1; 6-4-10: *Mannusaip perubāram nīnga ōr bharata mā perumpōr panni, mayangal seythu.*
36. *TVM*, 3-10-5.
37. *TVM*, 4-6.
38. *TVM*, 5-3.
39. *TVM*, 5-3.
39a. *TVM*, 6-7-1.
40. *PTM*, 1-3.
41. *PTM*, 1-4.
42. *PTM*, 1-5.
43. *PTM*, 1-6.
44. *PTM*, 1-7.
45. *PTM*, 1-8.
46. *PTM*, 2-1.

47. *PTM*, 2-2.
48. *PTM*, 2-3.
49. *PTM*, 2-4.
50. *PTM*, 2-5.
51. *PTM*, 2-7.
52. *PTM*, 2-8.
53. *PTM*, 2-10; 1-2.
54. *PTM*, 2-9-1.
55. *PTM*, 2-4-2.
56. *PTM*, 2-8-3.
57. *PTM*, 2-9-8.
58. *PTM*, 3-4.
59. *PTM*, 3-6.
60. *PTM*, 3-7; 3-8.
61. *PTM*, 4-2-6.
62. *PTM*, 4-8, 1-2.
63. *PTM*, 2-8-7; 2-7-7.
64. *PTM*, 1-5-7.
65. "*Kuḍathādal Kunrēduthōndal*"—commentary of Adiyarku Nallar.
66. *PTM*, 3-9.
67. *PTM*, 1-7-6.
68. *PTM*, 2-8-8.
69. *VP*, 5th Hamsa—13th chapter.
70. *TPV*, 3-4.
71. *TPV*, 24.
72. *NTM*, I.
73. *NTM*, I. V.4.
74. *NTM*, I. V.8.
75. *NTM*, VI, TM.
76. *NTM*, VI, TM, V.3.
    Antari-Chūṭṭa...
    When Durgā was born as a sister of Kṛṣṇa to Devaki, she just disappeared in the sky. Hence she is called *Antari.*
77. *Perumāḷ T.M.*, 6-4.
78. *Perumāḷ T.M.*, 6-7.
79. *Perumāḷ T.M.*, 7-3.
80. *Perumāḷ T.M.*, 7-9.
81. *Kōvil-Oḷugu*, p. 6.
82. *Periya T.M.*, 6-4.
83. *Periya T.M.*, 3-10-8:
    "*Kunrathal malai thaḍuttu kudamāḍu kūttan...*"

84. *Periya T.M.*, 7-5.
85. *Periya T.M.*, 5-8; 7-8.
86. *Ibid.*
87. *Periya T.M.*, 10-6-1.
88. *Periya T.M.*, *Chappāni Koṭṭutal.*
89. *Periya T.M.*, 11-5.
90. Kural: *Kadalanna Kāmattarāyirum, Māthar madalurār marrayār mēl.*
91. *PTM, Kōil poriyālē oṟṟindu kuḍikuḍi āṭchaiginrōm.*
92. *ARE*, No. 453 of 1906. Dated in A.D. 770.
93. *Guruparampara* of Pinbalgia Perumal Jiyar.
93a. *Pandiar Seppedugal Pattu.*
94. Vilavatti Mangalur, Pikira copper plate grants of the Pallava king Simhavarman all open with invocation slokas to '*Bhagavat*', *SII*, Vol. XII, No. 5.
95. *Seminar on Rājarāja Chōḷa*, Bombay, 1987, p. 109.
96. Raman, K.V., *op. cit.*
97. *ARE*, No. 3 of 1931-32.
98. *ARE*, No. 61 of 1892. I am quoting only a few here. There are plenty.
99. Āṇḍāḷ's *Vāraṇamayiram* describing her marriage with Kṛṣṇa is recited in a Vaiṣṇava wedding.
100. *BHP*, XI.5:38-40. For a detailed discussion of this view see F. Hardy, *op. cit.*, p. 486ff. Also Hardy, *op. cit.*, p. 637ff.
101. Singer, Milton, *Kṛṣṇa: Myths, Rites and Attitudes*, p. 26.

Chapter III

KṚṢṆA IN THE POST-BHAKTI RELIGION AND LITERATURE

Introduction

It is interesting to see how Kṛṣṇa theme continued to receive an honoured place in the hearts and minds of the Tamil poets, philosophers, preceptors and the common people. Numerous works in Tamil, Sanskrit and the *maṇipravāḷa* language have come down to us which sing the glory of Kṛṣṇa and his multi-faceted personality. These works can be reviewed under two categories: (1) works of the Vaiṣṇava preceptors (*āchāryas*) particularly their commentaries in the *maṇipravāḷa* style and (2) the other general works of non-religious nature. The first category is of specialised character found in the writings of Rāmānuja and his successors which constitute an important corpus and source for the Srī-Vaiṣṇava theology.

Srīvaiṣṇava Commentaries

The post-bhakti Vaiṣṇava religion in Tamilnāḍu was marked by the elaborate exposition and institutionalisation of the ideas and philosophy of the Āḻvārs. A galaxy of illustrious preceptors like Nāthamuni, Yāmunāchārya, Rāmānuja, Embār, Kurēsa, Parāsara Baṭṭar, Nanjiyar, Nampiḷḷai, Piḷḷai Lōkāchārya, Vedānta Dēsika, Manavāḷa Mahāmuni and a host of later scholars carried on the *bhakti* or the *bhāgavata* tradition and expounded its tenets through their voluminous commentaries (*vyākhyānas*) and discourses (*upanyāsas* or *pravachanas*) in the temples and the seminaries (*mathas*). Some of their works were written in Sanskrit, some in Tamil and yet others in the *maṇipravāḷa* style—a free mixture of Sanskrit and Tamil languages. If the sentiments of the Āḻvārs can be described as emotional *bhakti*, those of the Āchāryas can be described as intellectual discourse on *bhakti-mārga.*

In Tamil literary history, the period is often called 'the age of commentaries'. A series of brilliant commentaries were written by the successive generations each elaborating the inner meanings of the Tamil hymns of the

Āḷvārs. Great scholars as they were in Sanskrit and Tamil lore, they expounded the Tamil *prabandhas* and correlated and synthesised them with rich Sanskrit sources like the Vēdas, the Upanishads, the epics, the *purāṇas* and the *Bhagavat Gītā* in a very unique and delectable style called *maṇipravāḷa.* Their main idea was to enjoy and explain the depth and the beauty of Āḷvārs' Tamil hymns and the subtleties of their thought and expression. Rightly have they been called the Ubhaya vēdāntins, exponents of the Sanskrit and Tamil Vēdas. In their works too, we find Kṛṣṇa theme dominating as indeed it did in the works of the Āḷvārs. The *Bhagavat Gītā* and possibly the *Bhāgavata Purāṇa* in particular profoundly influenced them. They considered these works and also the *Rāmāyaṇa* as extolling the *bhakti* and *prapatti-mārga* (path of surrender)—the path shown by the Āḷvārs. Indeed, they treated them as *Saraṇāgati-granthas.* They gave new interpretations to the ancient works like the *Rāmāyaṇa,* the *Mahābhārata* and the *Gītā* in the light of the Tamil hymns of the Āḷvārs with emphasis on love, service, devotion and surrender. They were also keen to controvert Sankara's theory of attributeless God (*nirguṇa-brahmam*), theory of illusion (*māyā-vāda*), the path of knowledge (*jñāna-mārga*) and non-dualism (*advaita*). We see in the works of Rāmānuja a different theory based on the concepts of *Saguna-brahmam* (God with attributes), reality of the world, *bhakti-mārga* and qualified monism (*visiṣṭādvaita*). They also held the Tamil language as worthy of equal veneration and a worthy path to salvation. It is not our concern here to trace the history of Visiṣṭādvaita philosophy or its theology; we would endeavour to demonstrate how Kṛṣṇa and his teachings in the *Gītā* were central to their philosophy. Kṛṣṇa as a lovable and divine child looms large in the works of the Āḷvārs; but in the works of the *āchāryas,* this aspect is overshadowed by Kṛṣṇa as a supreme teacher of the *Bhagavat Gītā* and the quintessence of *Vēdānta.*

Nāthamuni (824-924)

The first among the Vaiṣṇava theologians of this period was Nāthamuni. He was a native of Kāṭṭumannārkōil (in South Arcot District) where there is an ancient temple for Kṛṣṇa as the shepherd king (*mannār*). Fascinated by the Tamil hymns of the Āḷvārs on the greatness of Viṣṇu, he was the first to collect and codify the hymns and arrange for their recital in some temples. He recognised their importance and extolled them as the Drāvida-Vēda.

Yāmuna (c. 953)

His name in Tamil Yamunaitturaivar means 'who is the lord of Yamunā' i.e. Kṛṣṇa. Grandson of Nāthamuni, he was also known as Āḷavandār. His name and his works show his devotion and reverence to Kṛṣṇa. He popularised the teachings of Kṛṣṇa through his well-known work *Gītāsangraha.* In another work *Āgamaprāmānya,* he ably espouses the cause of the Bhāgavatas and defends the validity of the Pāncharātra *āgamas* and temple worship against the criticisms from the pure Veidikas, the orthodox adherents of the Vēdic mode of worship.[1] His *Stōtraratna* is a poem of seventy stanzas in praise of Viṣṇu and the doctrine of self-surrender as the path to salvation. He lived in Srirangam during the middle of the 10th century. According to the Vaiṣṇava tradition, he is said to have chosen Rāmānuja to carry on his teachings. Rāmānuja was greatly influenced by his works.

Rāmānuja (1017-1137)

He is considered the greatest exponent of Sri Vaiṣṇavism and Visiṣṭādvaita philosophy. Following the footsteps of the Āḷvārs, he preached the liberal socio-religious tenets of Bhāgavatism and stood for the integration of the lower castes in the religious scheme. He was profoundly influenced by Kṛṣṇa's personality and teachings as attested by his brilliant Sanskrit works like the *Gītā-Bhāshya* and the *Gadyatraya.* He differed from Sankara's theory of *advaita* or non-dualism, *māyā vāda* (world as an illusion), *nirguṇabrahmam* (God without attributes) and put forth a strong argument for Visiṣṭādvaita.

According to him, the Brahmam or universal God is full of auspicious qualities and compassion and approachable by sincere devotion (*bhakti*) and concentration on the supreme personality and divine qualities of Lord Viṣṇu. Rāmānuja glorified the *Gītā* as it expounds the idea of *avatāra* the central idea of which is that God descends to earth in human form out of his love for humanity. He defines *bhakti* as that which comes through "discrimination, control of passions, habitual practice of religious disciplines, sacrifice, purity, strength and control of excessive joy". His sentiments show clearly the influence of the *Gītā* on Rāmānuja. According to his disciple Amudanār, who has written 100 verses in Tamil on Rāmānuja (*Rāmānuja-nūtrandādi*), he delved deep into the *Gītā* and brought out the essence of Kṛṣṇa's teachings for the benefit of humanity.[2] Every day, he used to recite the Tamil verses of Āṇḍāḷ's *Tiruppāvai* in praise of Kṛṣṇa and hence was known as Tiruppāvai-Jīyar.

All the works of Rāmānuja were written in Sanskrit and through them he could put across his philosophy to the whole of India. He could spread his Bhakti religion in North India, only through Sanskrit. Following Rāmānuja many Vaiṣṇava scholars wrote their works in Sanskrit.

Tiruvarangattu Amudanār

He was a disciple of Rāmānuja. He was doing daily service to Srirangam temple. In his *Rāmānuja-Nūtrandādi,* a Tamil work of great beauty, he speaks of the greatness of Kṛṣṇa as a source of solace and refuge for the good and the devoted. He points out how he went to the rescue of Dharma (Yudhiṣṭra) and his brothers (Pāṇḍavas) his ar‿ent devotees and protected them against the wicked Kauravas.[2a] In another verse he mentions how Rāmānuja was steeped in devotion to Kṛṣṇa and the Bhāgavata philosophy. He also pays tribute to Rāmānuja for disseminating the teachings of Kṛṣṇa.

Kūrattāḷvār

Kūrattāḷvār was a close associate of Rāmānuja and he wrote beautiful Sanskrit poems in praise of Viṣṇu. In his work *Adimānushastavam,* there are nearly 25 verses, dealing with Kṛṣṇa theme. The Pūtana episode, Sakaṭāsura-vadha and the felling of the *maruda* trees are extolled by him. He was also greatly impressed by the Lord's easy accessibility. The Āḷvār wonders how Kṛṣṇa who was beyond the comprehension of the *yogis* became such an earthly character as to steal butter in the houses of cowherds!

"Why Kṛṣṇa, who can rescue his devotees from the bonds of life and birth, allowed himself to be bound by a rope for stealing butter?"

The Āḷvār says, "The very aim of Kṛṣṇāvatāra was to show his quality of easy accessibility (*saulabhya*) hiding his supreme status (*paratva*)." He further asks him "why did you show your divinity in between like the lifting of the Gōvardhana hill when you wanted to hide it and be as human as possible?"

Kūrattāḷvār says: "There is one consoling fact for us who were not fortunate enough to see Kṛṣṇa and his sports. The places associated with him like the Yamunā river, Gōvardhana, Vrindāvana and Mathura can all be seen even now."

He laments that if he were born even as an inanimate object in Brindavan during Kṛṣṇa's time he would have escaped from the cycle of births.

In one of the concluding verses, the Āḷvār distinguishes Kṛṣṇa themes into two categories: the acts of heroism like Kamsa-vadha; and acts of humility. He says that the latter are always loved better by us.

His another work *Sundarabhāhustavam* deals with Kṛṣṇa theme at considerable length. The verses from 107 to 117 deal with Krishna theme. In an interesting analysis of Kṛṣṇa's life, he states that Kṛṣṇa had two mothers, and two fathers and belonged to two communities (*kulas*) and in that order two wives, one from the Kshatriya community (Rukmini) and another from the Yādavakula (Nappinnai). This is cited to show how deeply he was immersed in the analysis of Kṛṣṇa's life and teachings.

Parāsara Baṭṭar

Kūrattāḻvār's son was Baṭṭar. He lived in Srirangam and was well known for his brilliant discourses in the temple and his famous commentary on the *Viṣṇu-Sahasranāma.* Another important work of his was the *Rangarājastava* on Sri Ranganātha. Describing Lord Ranganātha's beautiful appearance, he refers to the ornaments that are adorning the Lord's chest and says along with his usual basil (*tulasi*) garland, *kaustuba* and the *Vaijayanthi-hāra* there are also some of the ornaments he wore during the time of Kṛṣṇāvatāra. He says *āmai-tāli, pulinagam* and *Panchāyuda-hāra* which were presented by Yasōdā to her son Kṛṣṇa, are still to be seen worn by Lord Ranganātha. These ornaments remind us of the Lord's humble origin and the folk customs. On the other hand, the other precious jewellery reminds us of his supreme divinity (*paratva*).

When Baṭṭar describes the greatness of the Lord's divine feet, he glorifies the feet which moved in Brindāvan. The tiny feet danced in Brindāvan according to the rhythmic sound of the churning of the curd by his mother. Above all, the feet when they are asked whether they would like to be placed on the heads of the Dēvas, or would they prefer to serve as a messenger to devotees, "they are readily willing to go as a messenger. They will dance in joy even at the thought of being a messenger of a devotee."

In another verse, Baṭṭar describes beautifully the effecṭ of Kṛṣṇa's flute on both living and non-living things. On hearing the sweet music played by Kṛṣṇa on the flute on the banks of the river Yamunā, the hard mountain became soft, fire became cold, the poison in the snakes began to disappear and in its place came the nectar, and above all, the ferocious tigers and the harmless cows were standing side by side. There was not a single thing which had not been touched and well ordered by the divine music.

Piḷḷai Perumāḷ Iyengār

He was a contemporary of Parāsara Baṭṭar, who lived in the 12th century A.D. His original name Aḻagiya Manavāḷa-dāsar was lovingly changed by the poet as Piḷḷai-Perumāḷ, 'the child-god' a significant name of Kṛṣṇa.

He has written *Ashta-prabandhas* consisting of eight separate works. Of these *Thiruvarangattu-mālai* speaks of Kṛṣṇa legends in about 25 stanzas. Kṛṣṇa the Almighty doing the humble and subservient role as a messenger of the Pāṇḍavas, dining at Vidura's place, protecting Draupati's chastity and teaching *Gītā* to Pārtha form the theme of these poetic outpourings. Iyengār also refers to a number of peculiar episodes related to Kṛṣṇa's boyhood. He refers to dance-forms namely *marakkāl-kūttu* or *poykkāl kūttu* performed by Kṛṣṇa.

He narrates an interesting story related to the birth of Balarāma and Kṛṣṇa. When the whole world was filled with sinners and demons, Bhūdēvi went and appealed to Nārāyaṇa. The Lord took out two hairs from his body, a white one and a black one and assured Bhūdēvi that they would be born to Dēvaki and save the earth. Thus the fair-coloured Balarāma and the dark-complexioned Kṛṣṇa were born on this earth.

Many fascinating episodes are told and retold about Kṛṣṇa, his various playful acts of stealing butter and ghee steal our hearts too. Here, Piḷḷai Perumāḷ Iyengār narrates yet another interesting story of Kṛṣṇa. A cowherd girl caught Kṛṣṇa stealing butter and with a rope tied him to a wooden mortar and went to Yasōdā to complain, taking her own child with her. When she just opened her mouth to report to Yasōdā, a strange thing happened. Her own child became Kṛṣṇa and in Kṛṣṇa's place was her child tied to the mortar!

In another verse, Iyengār says that when a cowherd woman beat Kṛṣṇa with a big wooden mallet, the whole universe which was kept safely inside his stomach was beaten.

There is another very interesting incident referred to by the poet. Kṛṣṇa, as usual, was found stealing butter by Yasōdā who wanted to punish him. Kṛṣṇa escaped from her, started running and Yasōdā was chasing him. On the way, Kṛṣṇa saw an old cowherd namely Dadhi Pāṇḍava having a huge mud pot (*thāḷi*) with him. Kṛṣṇa requested him to allow him to hide in the pot and asked him to tell Yasōdā that he had not seen Kṛṣṇa. Dadhi Pāṇḍava obliged and did so. The old man realising the true form of the supreme divinity thus agreed on the condition that Kṛṣṇa would give salvation in return not only to him but also to his kith and kin and even to the mud pot. Helpless Kṛṣṇa gave *mukti* to them all as wished for. Iyengār alludes to this beautiful episode which is mentioned in the *Brahma Vaivartapurāṇa* and also by Periyāḷvār.

Periyavāchān Piḷḷai

Periyavāchān Piḷḷai, known as "Vyākhyāna Chakravarti" (king of commentators) for his great contribution in the field of commentaries on the *Nālāyira Divya Prabandha.* He was born in A.D. 1228. He was a great devotee of Kṛṣṇa. His other names were Kṛṣṇa Pāda and Kṛṣṇa Sūri. In his commentaries, he establishes the superiority of the Bhāgavata-dharma through *bhakti,* over the Vēdic practices.

For instance, Periyavāchān Piḷḷai compares the Bhāgavatas to the tasty curd and the others to the insipid butter milk. While commenting on Kṛṣṇa's act of kicking the butter milk pot and eating the curd,[3] Periyavāchān Piḷḷai says, Kṛṣṇa does not like curd and the butter milk to be kept side by side and he accepts only the curd i.e. Bhāgavatas. This is only one of the numerous references to Kṛṣṇa's greatness found in his works.

Piḷḷai Lōkāchārya

Piḷḷai Lōkāchārya, son of Vadakku Thiruvīdi Piḷḷai, was another great Vaiṣṇava scholar who lived in Srirangam and wrote works like *Srīvachana-Bhūshana* and *Mummutchupadi* in the *maṇipravāḷa* style.

His work *Srīvachana-Bhūshana* contains brilliant exposition of the path of surrender (*Saraṇāgati-mārga*). He quotes from the *Rāmāyaṇa* and *Mahābhārata* to support his views. He cites the example of Draupati's total surrender to Kṛṣṇa when she was disrobed and humiliated in the court of the Kauravas and how Kṛṣṇa answered her prayers.

His work *Srīvachana-Bhūshana* consists of 461 *sūtras* and one of them states, "while *Rāmāyaṇa* speaks about the greatness of Sītā, who was imprisoned by Rāvaṇa, the *Mahābhārata* tells the greatness of Kṛṣṇa who accepted the humble role of a messenger."[4]

Vēdānta Dēsika (1268-1369)

Vēdānta Dēsika, a versatile scholar, poet and preceptor, lived in Kānchipuram in the middle of 13th-14th century. He was the author of over a hundred works both in Sanskrit and Tamil. His two Sanskrit works which are most relevant to our studies are the *Yādavābhyudayam* and *Gopālavimsati*, the former is a long *kāvya* and the latter is a shorter one with a string of 22 devotional songs.

Yādavābhyudayam

It is a *kāvya* on the lines of Kālidāsa's *Raghuvamsa*. It is also called *Kṛṣṇā-bhyudaya*. It has 24 cantos written in a variety of metres and imageries. It covers the life-history of Kṛṣṇa in great detail and each canto is devoted to an important episode like the birth of Kṛṣṇa, lifting of the Gōvardhana hill, killing of Kēsi and Kamsa, marriage with Rukmini and Satyabhāmā, Sisupāla-vadha, Narakāsura-vadha, marriage with 16,000 *gōpastris* (cowherd girls), his journey to Dwārakā, his preaching of the *Gītā* etc. The work holds a high place in the history of Sanskrit literature. It has a fine commentary also by Appaya Dīkshitar.

In his work Vēdānta Dēsika has followed the *nāyaka-nāyaki-bhāva* adopted by the Āḷvārs earlier. He says in a verse that the only feeling possible for a votary contemplating on Kṛṣṇa, the abode of infinite beauty and bliss, is the feeling a woman has for her lover. His work has been aptly described as a "love epic".[5] He has devoted a canto for the *rāsa-līlā* dance.

Vedānta Dēsika was equally inspired by Kṛṣṇa as a supreme teacher (*Gītāchārya*) as seen from his two works *Gītā-tātparya chandrika* and the *Gītārtha-Sangraharaksha*. The former is a commentary and defence of Rāmānuja's *Gītā Bhāshya* and the latter is a commentary on Yāmunāchārya's work *Gītārtha-Sangraha*.

Vēdānta Dēsika's *Gopālavimsati* is a shorter poem on Kṛṣṇa and is particularly noted for his description of the beauty of Kṛṣṇa's *navanīta-nāṭya* (butter-dance).

Manavāḷa Mahāmuni (1370-1443)

He was a renowned scholar in Sanskrit and Tamil. He was a native of the Pāṇḍyan country. He wrote a number of popular works. His commentary on Periyāḷvār's work *Tiruppallāṇḍu* is well known. Particularly incisive are his comments on Kṛṣṇa's playful acts at Gōkulam. He recalls one interesting incident. Once, Kṛṣṇa after having eaten all the butter kept in his house and without leaving any trace of the theft pretended to be asleep. His mother Yasōdā returned home and checked the stores and found the butter pots empty. Suspecting Kṛṣṇa as the culprit, she simply uttered the word "butter". Before she could complete her sentence, child Kṛṣṇa exclaimed "Mother, I have nothing to do with the theft" exposing his guilty conscience! Manavāḷa Mahāmuni draws on many such interesting incidents to make his commentary alive. His commentary is often quoted by the Srīvaiṣṇava scholars in their discourses on the *Bhāgavata*.

One important point may be noted in conclusion. The lively commentaries combined with the philosophy contained in the works of the Āchāryas mentioned above were not simply in the books to be read only by the learned. By a unique system of discourses (*upanyāsas*), which is kept alive to this day, they were disseminated to the wider public in the temple courtyard. Those discourses were largely attended by people of all castes and hence they served to popularise the tenets of the Āḷvārs, the Bhāgavata school and the Visiṣṭadvaita philosophy.

Other Works

Perundēvanār's Bhārata-Veṇba

Perundēvanār, a poet belonging to the times of Nandivarma Pallava III (9th century), wrote the *Bhāratam* in Tamil. Only 600 verses are available at present. The extant portions include the whole of the Udyōga and Bhishma-parvas and part of Drōna-parva. It consists of poems in *veṇba* metre interspersed with prose passages. His language and sentiments closely resemble those of the Āḻvārs. The poet was certainly influenced by the Bhakti cult centring around Kṛṣṇa and thus he echoes the same sentiments in many places. His description of Arjuna's surrender to Kṛṣṇa looks more like the Āḻvārs' approach to Kṛṣṇa. Epithets which are Vaiṣṇava in spirit like Māyavan, Emberumān and Kaḍalvaṇṇan are frequently used by Pērundēvanār also.

Like the Āḻvārs, the poet is captivated by simplicity of Lord Kṛṣṇa who went as a messenger to the Kaurava court. It is interesting to note that the poet follows the Āḻvārs in another aspect also of composing hymns in praise of the sacred temples. Each day of the Bhārata war begins with invocatory verses in praise of holy places like Tennarangam (Srirangam), Tirumalai (Tirupati), Tiruattiyūr (Kānchipuram) and Tirumālirunsōlaimalai.

In numerous places Perundēvanār praises Kṛṣṇa as the supreme Lord (*Paramporuḷ*). He glorifes him as the mother of the earth and space.[6] Like Nammāḻvār he also says that Kṛṣṇa is Wind, Fire, he is also Thunder, he is the Sun, he is the Vēdas, he is all the four directions and he is the very life of all the living things.[7]

Jayangondār's Kalingattuparaṇi

A war poem par excellence is the *Kalingattuparaṇi* written by Jayankondār the poet laureate of Kulōttunga Chōḷa I. It is considered as a masterpiece in Tamil literature known for its majestic style and diction. It vividly describes Kulōttunga's expedition to Kalinga (Orissa) and the victorious battles he won there. He aptly compares it with the *Mahābhārata* war and says Kṛṣṇa the hero of that war came as Kulōttunga to glorify the Sūrya-kula (Solar race) of the Chōḷas.

Srī Bhaṭṭanār's Paramārtha-Darsanam

The first ever translation of the *Bhagavat Gītā* into Tamil was written by Srī Bhaṭṭanār in the 13th century. The work was named as *Paramārtha-Darsanam.* The introductory verse says that Māyōn who preached the *Gītā* in Sanskrit was born in Chema-nagar as Bhaṭṭanār to render his own work into Tamil.[8] Two of the four invocatory verses sing in praise of Lord Kṛṣṇa as Pārthasārathi.

Villi-Bhāratam (c. A.D. 1400)

Villi-Bhāratam is a popular and major work in Tamil written by Villiputtūrār.

It is a beautiful re-rendering of the epic *Mahābhārata* story in a poetic form in more than 4300 verses. The author was born in Saniyur in Thirumunaippāḍi region in a Vaiṣṇavite family. His father was Veerarāghavachārya, a Vaiṣṇava Brahmin.

Villiputtūrār clearly states that his sole reason for writing the Bhārata story in Tamil is to have an opportunity to sing the glories of Kṛṣṇa (Mādhava) in the work. He begins each chapter with invocatory verses on Kṛṣṇa. His indebtedness to the Āḷvārs is evident from his reverential references to Thirumangai Āḷvār, Nammāḷvār and Thondaraḍipoḍi.

He frequently refers to many of the sports of Kṛṣṇa's childhood like Pūtana-vadha, Chakatasura-vadha, Kamsa-vadha, and also his later achievements like the bringing of the Pārijāta tree. The poet carefully remembers to refer to Nappinnai whom Kṛṣṇa married after subjugating seven bulls.

Like the Āḷvārs, Villiputtūrār too showers innumerable epithets in beautiful Tamil to describe Kṛṣṇa such as *Karumugil-vaṇṇan* (dark coloured), *Kamala-kaṇṇan* (the lotus eyed), *Kariya-Kōvalan* (black shepherd), *Yadhukula-nāyakan* (hero of yadhu-vamsa), Māyōn and Mēgaméniyān (one whose body is like the clouds). The poet, like the Āḷvārs, glorifies Kṛṣṇa as the supreme being, as the Lord of all the dēvas including Indra,[9] as the very seed for the Vēdas[10] and as the ultimate soul who is beyond even thousand Vēdas.[11]

This work occupies a high place in the history of Tamil literature for its rhythmic flow of the poetic language and eloquent comparisons, impressive imagery and dramatisation. Scholars have often compared this work with the *Kamba Rāmāyaṇa* for its epic style. In Tamilnāḍu, this Tamil version of the *Mahābhārata* has become so popular that its verses are freely used in the street dramas (*Theru-kūthu*) of the *Mahābhārata* regularly held in the villages. Particularly, the passages describing the Kurukshētra war which are couched in words sounding like the rattling of the chariot and the thundering of the war-drums are extremely popular in the street dramas which are seen and enjoyed by thousands of the village folks.

Oṭṭakkūthar

Oṭṭakkūthar was a court poet of the Chōḷa kings Vikrama Chōḷa, Kulōttunga II and Rājarāja II. His work *Mūvar-Ula* gives us historical facts of his period. *Ula* is one of the six main types of *prabandhas.* It sings about the seven stages of women and their love for the hero (here the king) when he is taken in a procession through the streets. The woman of *terivai* stage summons the street singers and asks them to enact the episodes of Kṛṣṇa's childhood. They play on the flute and dance as Kṛṣṇa did on the hoods of Kāliya and with the pots, recalling all the while the identification of the Chōḷa king with Kṛṣṇa. David Shulman says: "Thus the *terivai* and her bards sing of Kṛṣṇa, here the mythic model for the king (with the *gopis* cast in the role of the Chōḷa women), the latter is present in their minds as an ideal image of the lover who is nevertheless physically remote, unattainable at best, the substance of a dream."[12] Thus, even later poets followed the same tradition of equating their rulers with Lord Kṛṣṇa, the romantic hero.

The excerpts given above are only select examples to show how Kṛṣṇa theme was continuously handled by the Tamil poets and writers in different contexts. There are many more works which incidentally mention Kṛṣṇa and his greatness all of which cannot be presented here. For instance, the great Tamil poet Kamban in his immortal epic *Rāmāvatāra* (popularly called the *Kamba-Rāmāyaṇa*) refers to Kṛṣṇa in endearing terms as an *avatāra* of Viṣṇu. Similarly, Arunagirināthar who was an ardent devotee of Lord Muruga (or Subrahmaṇia) and sang such beautiful poems like *Tiruppugal, Kandar Alankāram,* etc. frequently pays his homage to Kṛṣṇa or Mādhava, the uncle of his favourite deity Muruga. This is an example to show how reverence to Kṛṣṇa transcended sectarian differences.

Subrahmaṇya Bhārati, considered the father of the renaissance movement in modern Tamil poetry, was a great devotee of Kṛṣṇa. His compositions on Kṛṣṇa in simple and mellifluous Tamil have become extremely popular in Tamilnāḍu. He described Kaṇṇan (Kṛṣṇa) as his inseparable companion and his beloved, his servant, his teacher, his God and composed songs on each one of these aspects. He has selectively translated the *Bhagavat Gītā* in Tamil and emphasised the action or Karma-yōga as the surest means to attain freedom from the British rule. He also wrote his famous long poem *Pānchāli-Sabdam* in which he dramatises Pānchāli or Draupadi's vow to avenge the humiliation done to her by Duryōdhana and his brothers. He compares Mother India to Pānchāli and the Duryōdhana brothers to the British rulers and beautifully interprets this epic episode in the context of India's struggle for freedom.

Thus from the Sangam age to Subrahmaṇya Bhārati, Kṛṣṇa's life and teachings have been a source of inspiration for the Tamil people at different levels —religious, philosophical and literary.

In the folk literature at the village level too the *Mahābhārata* and the *Rāmāyaṇa* are perhaps the most popular epic stories in Tamilnāḍu as indeed they are in the rest of India. We get numerous inscriptions referring to the endowments made to the temples for discourses or reading of the *Mahābhārata* in the temples. The rendering of the epic in Tamil by Perundēvanār in the 9th century and Villiputtūrār in the 15th century increased its popularity further. The Villiputtūrār *Bhāratam* even today holds the ground and is freely used in the street-dramas (*therukūthu*) in the villages. The village people are very much familiar with the characters of the epic and in fact the personal names of the people are very often after the noble characters of the epic like Kṛṣṇa, Balarāma, Arjuna, Dharma. Temples for Dharmarāja (Yudhiṣṭra) and his noble wife Draupadi or Pānchāli are to be found in numerous villages of Tamilnāḍu clearly indicating the widespread influence of the *Mahābhārata* epic and the life of Kṛṣṇa even at the folk level.

Kṛṣṇa Theme in Dance, Drama and Music

Kṛṣṇa's fascinating life and sports became favourite themes for musical compositions and dance forms. Particularly, the Kaveri basin became the cradle of interesting music and dance schools during the reigns of the Nāyak and Mahratta rulers (with Tanjavur as the capital) i.e. from 16th to 18th centuries. Many of the kings of these lineages, besides being patrons of arts and literature, were themselves scholars and music composers.

Vijayarāghava Nāyak (1634-1673) was a trend setter in the *yakṣagāna* dance and drama tradition. Among his twenty and odd dramas many were on Kṛṣṇa theme like *Kāliyamardana, Kṛṣṇa-Vilāsamu* and *Pūtana-Haraṇamu*. The famous composer Kshetrajna (1610-1685) stayed in his court and composed several of his *padas*, popular in carnatic music and dances. As pointed out by B. Natarajan, the family deity of Tanjavur Nayaks was Rājagōpāla (Kṛṣṇa) of Mannarkudi in Tanjavur district. Sahaji II, the Mahratta ruler of Tanjavur, was another prolific composer and he wrote several *kritis* on many deities including Rājagōpāla of Mannarkudi.[13]

The Melattur Bhāgavata-Mēla and the Bhajana-sampradāya traditions that became strong in Tanjavur region in places like Melattur, Varahur, Uttukkadu and Sulamangalam deserve special mention. Great exponents of Nāmasankīrtana tradition like Sridhara Ayyāvāḷ of Tiruvisainallur, Bodhēndrasvāmi, Sadāsiva Brahmēndra composed serveral *Kīrtanas* on Kṛṣṇa which became very popular.

Another leading luminary was Nārāyaṇa Tīrtha (1675-1745) who wrote his famous work *Srikṛṣṇa-leela-Tarangiṇi* (*The River of Kṛṣṇa's Sports*) in classical Sanskrit in twelve *tarangas* like the twelve chapters of Jayadeva's *Gīta-Gōvinda*. He hailed from Andhra but settled down in Tamilnāḍu at Varahur, near Tanjavur. The work gives a condensed version of the *dasamaskandam* of the *Srīmad Bhāgavatam* from Kṛṣṇa's birth to his marriage with Rukmini. It consists of rhythmic *Kirtanas, gadyas* and *darus* sung in nearly forty *rāgas*. Under his own guidance, it was enacted as dance-drama every year during the Gōkulāṣṭami day in the Venkatēsa-perumāḷ temple at Varahur. The *uriyaḍi*

88. Kṛṣṇa-līlā paintings, Kānchipuram.

89. Kṛṣṇa-līlā paintings, Tirupparuttikunram.

90. Kṛṣṇa with the gōpis, Srīrangam.

91. Kṛṣṇa with the gōpis, Srīrangam.

92. Kṛṣṇa with butter pot, Thanjavur.

93. Kṛṣṇa with the gōpis, ivory carving, Srīrangam.

94. Rāsa-līlā scenes, ivory carving, Srīrangam.

95. Kṛṣṇa with butter pot, wood carving, Mannārguḍi.

96. Kṛṣṇa killing Pūtaki, Mannārguḍi.

97. Kṛṣṇa killing Kuvalayapita (elephant), Mannārguḍi.

98. Kṛṣṇa and Arjuna in the chariot, Mannārguḍi.

99. Wood-carvings, Pūtaki-vadha and Kṛṣṇa-līlā scenes, Kānchi.

100. Yasōda-Kṛṣṇa (metal), Chennai Museum.

festival on the occasion attracts large crowds. Songs selected from the opera became an integral part of the Bhajana tradition of South India.

Nārāyaṇa Tīrtha also wrote a drama named *Pārijātapaharaṇa Nāṭaka.* His *tarangini* had inspired many later composers including the great music celebrity Saint Thyagaraja (according to Dr. V. Raghavan).[14]

Another noted and influential composer of the Bhāgavatamēla tradition was Uttukkadu Venkaṭa-kavi (1700-1762). The idol of Kṛṣṇa in the temple of his village Uttukkadu was his patron deity and he composed nearly two hundred songs in Tamil and Sanskrit especially on Rādhā and Kṛṣṇa. His Tamil songs couched in simple and rhythmic style have become favourite items in the carnatic music and dance performances (songs like *tāyē yasōdē, alai-pāyudē* etc.). Uttukkadu came to be known to the devotees as the Southern Gōkulam.

In the early decades of the last century, i.e. in pre-cinema era, street and stage dramas became popular in Tamilnāḍu and here again the puranic themes like *Kṛṣṇa-leelā, Kṛṣṇa-tūtu, Alliarasāni-mālai, Chitrāngada-kathai, Pavaḷakkoḍi* became popular.

In the early decades of the cinema era also, the puranic themes dominated. Several movies based on Kṛṣṇa theme were made like *Bhakta Kuchēla, Kṛṣṇa-tūtu, Kṛṣṇa-bhakti, Haridas, Meera* and *Sri Kṛṣṇa-Tulābharam.* A most renowned exponent and composer of carnatic music Sangita Kalānidhi Pāpanasam Sivan had composed the songs for many of the movies mentioned above and they became great musical hits.

In the more recent decades, another illustrious and widely acclaimed Tamil poet who wrote popular songs on Kṛṣṇa for cinema was Kannadāsan. An activist in the Dravidian movement and an agnostic in his earlier days, he became a great devotee and admirer of Kṛṣṇa and assumed the name Kannadāsan (servant of Kṛṣṇa).

References

1. *Āgama Prāmanya,* ed. Misra Sastri, pp. 6-10.

2. *Rāmānuja Nūtrandādi,* verse 68.

2a. *Ibid.*

3. This idea is also found in *Siria-Thirumaḍal* of Tirumangai Āḷvār: "...*Ārādha vennai vilungi arugiruntha morōr kuḍamuruṭṭi*".

4. *Srī Vachana Bhūṣanam,* 5th sutra.

5. Satyavrata Singh, *Vedanta Desika, His Life, Works and Philosophy,* 1958, p. 473.

6. *Bhārata-Veṇba,* v. 124.

7. *Bh.,* V.135. This reminds us of a similar well-known verse in Nammāḷvār's *Tiruvāymōḷi* expressing same sentiments (*Tiruvāymōḷi*: 3-4).

8. *Chēya mā madurai ninrum*
   Chemama nagaru tēḍi
   Āyanar Bhattanaray
   Avadaritharuḷina...
   See M. Arunachalam, *History of Tamil Literature.*
9. *V.Bh., Sambava-charukkam,* V.114.
10. *V.Bh., Āraṇya Parvam, Arjunan Tavanilai Charukkam;* V.8.
11. *V.Bh., Virāṭa-Parvam, Nadukarandurai Charukkam,* V.1.
12. Shulman, D.D., *The King and the Clown in South Indian Myths and Poetry*, pp. 685-86.
13. B. Natarajan, *Srī Kṛṣṇa Tarangini by Nārāyaṇa Tīrtha,* p. 20.
14. *Ibid.*

Chapter IV

TEMPLES OF KṚṢṆA IN TAMILNĀḌU—TRADITIONS AND HISTORY

Introduction

In this section we identify temples specifically dedicated to Kṛṣṇa in different parts of Tamilnāḍu and trace their history and tradition. Among them some are very ancient and found mentioned in the Sangam literature, some others came into prominence during the Bhakti period (7th and 8th centuries A.D.) and many more came up during the Chōḷa and Vijayanagar times. We see a remarkable continuity of tradition in that the sacred temples continued to receive the patronage and the devotion of the kings and the common people, for centuries without any break. Each generation took pride in fostering the care of the temple and trying to add some new facets to the temple by way of construction of some shrines or *maṇḍapas* or introducing some new festivals or services and, on the whole, maintaining and improving the existing facilities of Kṛṣṇa worship. Since this survey involves a fairly long period, we can trace the history of the Kṛṣṇa shrines of Tamilnāḍu regionwise; that is to say, regions traditionally considered to be the territorial components of Tamilnāḍu for convenience, namely, *Toṇḍai-nāḍu, Pāṇḍya-nāḍu, Naḍu-nāḍu* and *Chōḷa-nāḍu* and *Kongu-nāḍu.*

For the history of a few shrines, we have to rely only on the literary and traditional accounts, as for instance, the temples mentioned in the Sangam literature. Some of them continue to be centres of worship still while some others are no longer to be seen and yet a few others have undergone re-designation and modification. But, from the 7th century onwards, not only the literary evidences become more copious in the form of the Bhakti literature, discussed in the earlier chapter, but we begin to get a new and valuable source-material, namely, the inscriptional evidence. The significance of the inscriptions can hardly be exaggerated. They are found *in situ* on the very walls of the temples in which Kṛṣṇa is enshrined. Secondly, they are fairly well dated, since they mention the kings in whose reign they were written. Moreover, the palaeography of the inscriptions has also enabled the epigraphists to fix the date fairly correctly. Another important aspect of the inscriptions is that they are not purely religious and therefore give us a good insight into the administrative transactions of the temple and management of the endowments and the different social groups and communities that were associated with the shrines. The inscriptions discussed in the chapter belong to a fairly long period from about 7th century to 17th century, belonging to different dynasties. They provide us with very valuable evidence regarding the patronage that the Kṛṣṇa temples received from the royal personages, merchants and other common people, the temple rituals and festivals that were introduced from time to time, the grant of lands, gifts of jewels, money and the like for specific purposes like celebration of festivals and institution of services in honour of the kings and welfare of the state.

Whereas in the purely religious literature, we hardly get information on the secular or social aspects, the inscriptional evidence provides us with the missing link and gives us a better perception of the relationship between the temples and the society. Apart from the association of the kings, nobles and the elite, it is through inscriptions that we get a clearer picture about the involvement of the different strata of society like the agriculturalists, the merchants, the shepherd class (the *manrāḍis*), the artists like the *dēvaradiyār* and the artisans. In this chapter more than 200 inscriptions are collected and examined in depth and the data collected from them is presented in a historical framework.

The diffusion of Pancha-vīra cult i.e. the *vyuha* form had taken place in Tamilnāḍu even during the Sangam period, as already pointed out. We see its impact on some temples like the Parthasarathi temple, Chennai, the temple at Nācchiyār Kōil (Tanjavur district) and the shrine on the hillock at Tiruttangal (Virudhunagar Dt.). These three early temples were built between 7th and 8th centuries A.D. But the Pancha-vīra cult almost lost its popularity in the Tamil country by about 9th century A.D. giving way to the *avatāra* concept. Temples were built for Viṣṇu in general and also for his various manifestations such as Rāma, Kṛṣṇa, Varāha and Narasimha in particular. Among the Vṛṣṇi heroes, except for Kṛṣṇa, all the others lost their importance and Balarāma, in particular, though considered as an incarnation of Viṣṇu was outshone by Kṛṣṇa. The switchover from the *vyuha* to the *vibhava* form in Tamilnāḍu was the outcome of the Bhakti movement of the Āḷvārs.

Toṇḍai-Nāḍu

Toṇḍai-Nāḍu comprises the erstwhile districts of Chengalpattu, South Arcot, North Arcot besides the region round Chennai. This territory can almost be called the nerve-centre of Tamil Bhakti movement since the first four Āḷvārs hailed from this region. This area was for a long time under the rule of the Pallavas who had their capital at Kānchi. There are many ancient and sacred shrines for Kṛṣṇa in this area and we will review their history one by one.

(1) Tirumalai-Tirupati

Though Tirumalai-Tirupati group of temples is now in Andhra Pradesh it was very much in Tamilnāḍu and considered as the northern limit of Tamilnāḍu and hence for convenience sake it has been included in this category. It was known to ancient Tamil literature as Vēngadam. Venkatēsvara, the Lord of Vēngadam, is traditionally regarded as an incarnation of Kṛṣṇa. According to the *Venkatesvara-Mahatmiyam* the Lord described himself to Goddess Padmāvati as Kṛṣṇa the eighth son of Dēvaki and Vāsudēva, as the brother of Balarāma and Subhadra, and as a friend of the Pāṇḍavas. It is also stated that after being shot at by a hunter and casting off his mortal coils, Kṛṣṇa emerged in the Sūryamaṇḍala in the form in which the image of Venkatēśvara is sculptured. Vaiṣṇava saints (Āḻvārs) who have sung many beautiful hymns on the Lord of Vēngadam often address him as Kṛṣṇa and attribute all the qualities of the latter. In the Gōvindarāja temple, Tirupati there is a separate shrine for Kṛṣṇa as Pārthasārathi. According to the local tradition, it was the original shrine that existed even before the establishment of the Gōvindarāja shrine. An inscription[1] of A.D. 1495 refers to the celebration of Kṛṣṇa's birthday (Jayanti) in the temple. In the nearby temple at Tiruchānur, there is a shrine for Rājagōpāla and his consorts Rukmini and Satyabhāmā.

(2) Pārthasārathi Temple, Tiruvallikēṇi, Chennai

The temple dedicated to Kṛṣṇa as Pārthasārathi is said to have been built during the Pallava period. This is one of the few Pancha-vīra temples in Tamilnāḍu. The temple has been sung by Pēyāḻvār, Tirumaḻisai-āḻvār and Tirumangai, the first two belonged to 7th century A.D. and the latter to 8th century.

In this temple, we see the whole Vṛṣṇi family consisting of Kṛṣṇa, Rukmini, Balarāma, Pradyumna, Aniruddha and Sātyaki is worshipped in the sanctum. The *mūla-mūrti* is known as Vēnkaṭa Kṛṣṇa and the *utsava-mūrti* is called Pārthasārathi. The *Sthalapurāṇa* goes like this: once a king called Sumati worshipped Tiruvēnkatamuḍaiyān, the Lord of Tirupati and pleaded with the Lord to give him the *darshan* as Pārthasārathi, the charioteer of Arjuna. The Lord obliged and gave *darshan* to his devotee as Pārthasārathi having *sankha* in his right hand and *varada-mudrā* in his left hand. Hence, the name *Vēnkaṭa-Kṛṣṇa.* The *utsava-mūrti* has four arms with *sankha, chakra,* a stick and *abhaya-mudrā.*

Tirumangai Āḻvār specifically praises the services rendered by a Pallava king in the construction of the temple and its *maṇḍapas.* This can be taken as a reference to king Nandivarman or his son Dantivarman, who were ardent devotees of Viṣṇu. An inscription dated 808 A.D. of the Pallava king Dantivarman registers a gift to the temple.[2]

The temple continued to receive substantial patronage in the Chōḷa and Vijayanagar times. A Vijayanagar inscription dated in the 16th century mentions the addition of a *maṇḍapa* like the *Tiruvāymōḷi-maṇḍapa*. Even today, this temple is a very busy and popular one in the city of Chennai, pulsating with festivals all through the year.

(3) Varadarājaswāmi Temple, Kānchipuram

There is a separate shrine for Kṛṣṇa near the main entrance opposite to the hundred pillared *maṇḍapa*. The architectural style suggests that it belonged to the later Pāṇḍya period. A fragmentary Tamil epigraph belonging to the late 13th century is found on the sanctum wall. An inscription of Kṛṣṇadēvarāya states that while the king was camping at Kānchi, two small cars for Gaṇēsa in Ekambaranātha temple and for Kṛṣṇa in the Perumāḷ temple were offered.[3] There are also inscriptions referring to the celebration of *Srī-Jayanti* (Kṛṣṇa's birthday) and *Uriyaḍi* festivals in this temple.[4]

(4) Pāṇḍava-Dūta Temple (Pāḍagam), Kānchi

Among the Viṣṇu temples at Kānchi sung by the Āḷvārs, the Pāṇḍava-Dūta temple is dedicated to Kṛṣṇa, as the messenger of the Pāṇḍavas. The temple was known as Pāḍagam in Āḷvārs' hymns. Totally six verses by Bhūtatāḷvār, Pēyaḷvār, Tirumalisai and Tirumangai are dedicated to this temple. As has already been mentioned, the great quality of easy accessibility of the Lord is always highlighted in the hymns of the Āḷvārs. This is exemplified by his role as a humble messenger or even as a charioteer to help his friends. The same idea is reflected in this temple where Kṛṣṇa is depicted in his *Visvarūpa* form which he took at the court of the Kauravas when Duryōdhana tried to kill him. According to the temple myth, king Janamejaya hearing the *Mahābhārata* from Vysampāyana wanted to see Kṛṣṇa in his Visvarūpa form shown at the court of Hastinapur. The king came to Kānchi and performed *aṣvamēdha.* Kṛṣṇa as Pāṇḍava-dūta came and accepted the offering. The stucco figure of seated Kṛṣṇa is in unusually tall and gigantic form. The processional deity is flanked by his consorts Rukmini and Satyabhāmā. We have some Chōḷa inscriptions of Kulōttunga I and Rājadhirājadēva II, registering gifts made to the temple.

The Vaikunta Perumal Temple at Kānchi, built by Nandivarman II Pallava (731-796), was built according to the Pāncharātra Āgama and as shown by Dennis Hudson, it was designed as a "visual summa of the *Bhāgavata Purāṇa*"[4a] (see also Chapter V).

(5) Rājagōpāla Perumāḷ Temple, Maṇimangalam

Maṇimangalam is a small village near Tambaram in the Chengalpattu district. The place Maṇimangalam was the site of one of the battles between the Pallava king Narasimhavarman I and the western Chalukyan Pulakesin II. There are three temples of Viṣṇu in Maṇimangalam namely Rājagōpālaswāmi, Vaikuṇṭa Perumāḷ and Kṛṣṇasvāmin. The Chōḷa inscriptions mention this village as Maṇimangalam in Tamil and as Ratnagrāma and Ratna-agrahāra in Sanskrit.

The date of the construction of the temple for Rājagōpāla is not certainly known. The temple has not been referred to by Āḷvārs. So, we can assume that it was built after the Bhakti period, perhaps in the 10th century. The Chōḷa inscriptions of this temple refer to the deity as Srimad-Dvarāpatidēva,[5] Vantuvarāpati Emberumān[6] (Lord of Dwārakā) and as Mannanār.[7] An inscription of the time of Rājēndra I dated in 1056 A.D. refers to the temple as *Kamakōṭi-viṇṇagar* thus associating Kāma (Aniruddha) with Kṛṣṇa. The temple is also referred to as *Tiruvāykulam.* The inscription gives information about the gifts and tax-free land grants made to the temple by private persons.[8]

Some of the Chōḷa inscriptions from the Vaikuṇṭa Perumāḷ temple in the same village are available to us.[9] An inscription of the time of Rājarāja I dated in the year 990 A.D. records gift of 90 sheep for a perpetual lamp in the temple of Tiruvāypāḍi Kṛṣṇa Perumāḷ, by one Edukilai Singamanrāḍi, a resident of the village.[10] He belonged to the cowherd community (*manrāḍi*) which took active interest in building and maintaining temples for their family deity, Kṛṣṇa. Another inscription of Kulōttunga I's period in the same temple registers gift of land by the members of the assembly of the Maṇimangalam village to the temple of Tiruvāypāḍi (Gōkulam).[11] From the inscriptions cited above it is seen that the Kṛṣṇa temple was patronised by the Brahmins as well as other classes especially the shepherd class.

(6) Uttaramērūr

Uttaramērūr, a village in Chengalpattu district, came into limelight in the middle of 8th century A.D. as a Brahmin settlement, a chaturvēdimangalam under the patronage of the Pallava king Nandivarman. It was predominantly a Vaiṣṇava settlement centring round a Viṣṇu temple. The various constituents of Uttaramērūr were named after the twelve names of Viṣṇu such as (1) Kesava-chēri, (2) Nārāyaṇa-chēri, (3) Mādhava-chēri, (4) Gōvinda-chēri, (5) Viṣṇu-chēri, (6) Madhusūdana-chēri, (7) Trivikrama-chēri, (8) Vāmana-chēri, (9) Srīdhara-chēri, (10) Hrishikesa-chēri, (11) Padmanābha-chēri and (12) Dāmōdara-chēri.[12]

Sundaravarada Perumāḷ temple is the main Viṣṇu temple of Uttaramērūr. The temple is located as per the prescription given in *Marichi-Samhitā.*[13] The temple is a Navamūrti-pratiṣṭa, having nine images consecrated. They are: Kṛṣṇa, Viṣṇu, Rāghava, Matsya, Kūrma, Baladēva, Kalki, Vāsudēva and Panchavīra.

The temple has a three-tier *vimāna* with a shrine in each storey, with standing, seated and reclining forms of Viṣṇu respectively in the first, second and third floor. An inscription of Rājarāja I (3rd year) records the setting up of the image of Tiruvāykulam-Udaiyān (Kṛṣṇa).[14] The temple is said to have been worshipped by the Pancha Pāṇḍavas. Several other images of Kṛṣṇa named as Tiruvāypaḍi-dēvar, Kurukshētra-dēvar, Gōvardhana-dēvar and Brindāvana-dēvar are mentioned.[15] They were evidently installed either in the Sundaravarada Perumāḷ Temple or Vaikuṇṭa Perumāḷ Temple of the village.

(7) Kari Kṛṣṇa Perumāḷ Temple, Tiruvāypāḍi

The name of the village is Tiruvāypāḍi (i.e. the sacred Gōkulam) in the Chengalpattu district. The presiding deity of the temple here is called Kari Kṛṣṇa Perumāḷ. It is datable to the Chōḷa period as it contains Chōḷa inscriptions.

(8) Vēnugōpālaswāmi Temple, Mēlpāḍi (North Arcot District)

The temple seems to have been built by the Chōḷa rulers and additions were made by the Zamindars of Karvettinagar in the 19th century. The principal deity is Vēnugōpālaswāmi with his two consorts.

(9) Vēnugōpālasvāmi Temple at Kaliappeṭṭai (Chengalpattu Dt.)

This is a village on the western bank of the river Pālar in Chengalpattu taluk. It is also called Doḍḍayachārpuram where Sri Vaiṣṇava Brahmin settlement was established in the 17th century A.D. The temple is dedicated to Kṛṣṇa as Vēnugōpāla. Regular annual festivals are taking place in which all the residents of the village participate actively. Residents of the village name their children after the village deity such as Venugōpālan, Kṛṣṇan etc.

(10) Tirumukkūḍal

In the Venkatēsa Perumāḷ temple in Tirumukkūḍal in the district of Chengalpattu, there is an inscription of Rājēndra I dated in his 11th year which registers a gift of 113 sheep to Veṇṇai-kūttar (Dancing Kṛṣṇa).[16]

(11) Sirudavūr

In this small village in the Chengalpattu district, we get Chōḷa inscription of the time of Rājēndradēva II dated around 1060 A.D. in the Viṣṇu temple. It registers a gift of land by Pudali Daṇḍaya Kramavittan for offerings and lamp to the image of dancing Kṛṣṇa (*Veṇṇaiku-kūttaḍuvār*) set up by himself in the Viṣṇu temple of the village.

(12) Tirumālpura

This is a place in North Arcot district. The name itself means 'Town of Viṣṇu'. Some very interesting inscriptions have come to us from this town. They are found in the ruined Viṣṇu temple located here. A Chōḷa inscription of 11th century registers the provision made for a lamp for the deity in the temple of Govindapāḍi by a Vellāḷa. The Sanskrit portion refers to the deity as *Kamsāri*, queller of Kamsa, i.e. Kṛṣṇa.[17]

Another Chōḷa inscription of 995 A.D. from the same temple records gift of gold by one Arumilai to Sri Kṛṣṇa. A Tamil hymn (*tiruppadiyam*) beginning with *Kōlanār-kuḷal* composed by the donor's father in praise of Kṛṣṇa (Gōvinda pāḍiāḷvār) had to be sung on the occasion of a festival.[18]

(13) Kariya Perumāḷ Temple, Athi (North Arcot District)

An inscription of 1268 A.D. found in the temple at Athi records gift of land by Rājarāja Sāmbuvaraya to the shrine of *Veṇṇaikkādiyarulina piḷḷai* (the boy who danced for butter).

(14) Venugōpālaswāmi Temple, Kalambūr (North Arcot District)

An inscription of 960 A.D. found in the temple of Venugōpālaswāmin records gift of lamps to the temple of Kalikēsari Viṇṇagardēvar by the assembly of Kalambūr.[19]

(15) Uttiraranganāthaswāmi Temple, Pallikonda (North Arcot District)

There is a separate shrine for Kannapiran opposite to the western *Gōpura*. The image is beautifully carved. Navanita Kṛṣṇa has butter balls in both his hands and places a leg on a churner. On Kṛṣṇa Jayanti day the idol is taken out in procession. *Uriyadi* festival is also celebrated[20] and the local shepherd community takes a leading part.

(16) Vrinchipuram (North Arcot District)

An interesting inscription of Vijayanagar king Dēvarāya dated in 1425 A.D. has come down to us to indicate the exalted position held by the Kṛṣṇa temple at Vrinchipuram. It registers an agreement signed by the Brahmins of the village in the presence of the deity Gopinātha (the Lord of the shepherds) at Vrinchipuram to the effect that marriages among themselves should be conducted only as *Kanyādāna* and not by giving or taking gold as prize money.

(17) Pulivalam (North Arcot District)

An inscription found in Pulivalam below the image of Vēnugōpālaswāmin sculptured on a slab set up near a tank is dated in Saka 1358 (1436 A.D.). It states that the tank was constructed by Rangarāja, son of Sāḷuva Annāmalairāja in the name of (God) Gopināthadēva.

(18) Tiruvattiyūr (North Arcot District)

An interesting inscription from Tiruvattiyūr gives the eulogy of the shepherd clan called Nandaputras or Vantuvarāpati Tiruvāypāḍi Nāṭṭāḷvār settled in Tondaimandalam. It states that the community met in the hall of the temple and expressed their gratitude for the divine grace shown on the caste and family.

(19) Vēṇugōpālaswāmi Temple, Kastambadi (North Arcot District)

This temple of Vēṇugōpāla can be ascribed to the late Vijayanagar times. An inscription here records the installation of the *Garudastambha.*[21]

(20) Ennāyiram (North Arcot District)

An inscription dated in the 13th regnal year of Rājādhirāja Chōḷa I found on the wall of Aḷagiya Narasimha Perumāḷ temple in Ennāyiram, near Villupuram registers that the great assembly of Rājarāja-Chaturvēdimangalam ordered that the lands of the temple of Tiruvāypāḍidēvar (Kṛṣṇa) be taxed at the lowest scale.[22]

Chōḷa-Nāḍu

(1) Pundarikāksha Temple, Tiruvellarai (Tiruchi District)

The most significant Pallava temple for Kṛṣṇa is the one at Tiruvellarai, very near Srirangam. Periyāḷvār and Tirumangai have sung about this temple. Periyāḷvār has dedicated a whole decad called '*Kāppu Parvam*' to Kṛṣṇa of Tiruvellarai. This is the temple where we find the earliest inscriptional evidence for Kṛṣṇa worship in Tamilnāḍu. We get reference to the installation and worship of the images of Kṛṣṇa and Rukmini by the Pallava king Dantivarman (796-847 A.D.).[23] Another inscription dated in the 8th regnal year of Uttama Chōḷa (c. 978 A.D.) registers the gift of gold made to Kṛṣṇa and his consort Rukmini by the Chōḷa princess Irayiravandēvi (wife of Rājādhittan, son of the Chōḷa king Parāntaka I).[24]

The images installed by Dantivarman are not to be seen in the temple at present, and the temple is generally known as Pundarikāksha temple. But there are ample sculptural evidences to show that it continued to be the centre of Kṛṣṇa worship. Kṛṣṇāyaṇa scenes in sculpture are available in plenty (cf. Chapter V). A bronze image of Kṛṣṇa is placed in the sanctum and on every Kṛṣṇa-Jayanti day, it is taken out in procession and worshipped. In a separate shrine in the *prākāra* are placed the stone images of Vēṇugōpāla with two consorts. On the walls of the "Swastika tank" built by Dantivarman, Kṛṣṇa's childhood sports are depicted in stone. The paintings of Kṛṣṇa are to be seen in the *Chitra-maṇḍapa*, and inside the sanctum sanctorum.

(2) Nācchiyār Kōil (near Kumbakonam, Thanjavur Dt.)

This is one of the few rare temples dedicated to Panchavīras. In the main shrine of the temple are placed the images of Sankarṣaṇa (Balarāma), Vāsudēva (Kṛṣṇa), Pradyumna, Aniruddha and Purushōttama along with the consort of Kṛṣṇa. The temple, originally called as Tirunarayūr, has been glorified by the Āḷvārs. This temple belongs to the late Pallava period.[25]

According to the *Sthalapurāṇa*, Vāsudēva came here and married Vanjuḷavalli, the adopted daughter of Madāvi rishi. The Lord assumed five forms namely Sankarṣaṇa, Vāsudēva, Pradyumna, Aniruddha and Purushōttama and married Vanjuḷavalli. The Lord is depicted as holding the hand of his consort.

(3) Ranganātha Temple, Srīrangam (Tiruchi Dt.)

Considered as the holiest of the holy shrines for the Vaiṣṇavas, it has been sung by almost all the Āḷvārs. Though the presiding deity is Lord Ranganātha in the reclining posture, many Āḷvārs and particularly Nammāḷvār have praised the temple as the abode of Kṛṣṇa. There are many Kṛṣṇa shrines in the temple premises. The main temple of Srirangam (or Tiruvarangam) is mentioned in the Sangam literature. The surrounding shrines are later additions in subsequent times. We can have a look at the shrines of Kṛṣṇa briefly.

(i) *Kṛṣṇa Shrine in the Kili-Maṇḍapa*

In the first inner enclosure, close to the main sanctum and facing west is the shrine for Kṛṣṇa. Here, the *utsavabēra* is Kṛṣṇa as *Navanīta-nritta-mūrti* or dancing Kṛṣṇa with a butter ball in his right hand. Just behind it, a stone image of Vāsudēva Kṛṣṇa can be seen. He is holding a vessel in his right hand and conch in the left. He is accompanied by his two consorts, Rukmini and Saytabhāmā. The location of the shrine close to the main shrine shows the importance given to Kṛṣṇa worship in this temple. The shrine belongs to the Chōḷa period.

(ii) *Pārthasārathi Shrine*

This shrine is located in an outer *prākāra* adjoining Rāmānuja's shrine. The stone image of Kṛṣṇa with two arms is in standing pose on a chariot. His left hand holds a whip and his right hand shows the *Vyākhyāna-mudrā.* Arjuna is shown standing beside with his hands in *anjali-mudrā.* The scene depicts Kṛṣṇa as Gītāchārya who taught the *Gītā* to Arjuna in the Kurukshētra battle-field.

In the same shrine are kept two stone images of Nara and Nārāyaṇa, representing Arjuna and Kṛṣṇa in their former births. Nārāyaṇa holds a whip in one hand and *Vyākhyāna-mudrā* in another. The processional deities are Kṛṣṇa and his two consorts Rukmini and Satyabhāmā.

(iii) *Viṭṭala Shrine*

It is located opposite to Āṇḍāḷ shrine in the outer *prākāra* known as the *Ranga-maṇḍapa.* Two-armed standing image of Kṛṣṇa is the presiding deity. It might have been built during the time of Vijayanagar or Nāyak kings who were devotees of Viṭṭala, another form of Kṛṣṇa famous in Mahārāshtra and popularised in Karṇāṭaka and Tamilnāḍu during the Vijayanagar times (15th-16th centuries).

(iv) *Vēnugōpāla Shrine*

This architecturally beautiful shrine for Vēnugōpāla was built during the time of the Hoysalas. The inscription which is dated 1154 A.D. states that the shrine was consecrated by Umādēvi, the queen of the Hoysala king Vīra Ballāḷa of Dwārasamudra.[26] It also records a gift of land for offerings to the God during the early morning service by Srimāra Bhaṭṭa to the temple of Tirukkuḻal-Ūdinapiḷḷai (Kṛṣṇa). This expressive Tamil term means 'the divine child who played with flute'. Another Hoysala inscription of 1270 A.D. registers an endowment of 100,000 *kāśu* for daily offerings to Tirukuḻal-Ūdina-Piḷḷai and his consorts by Aḷagiya Manavāḷa Bhaṭṭar.[27] The architecture of the shrine also shows Hoysala features. There are also beautiful paintings of Kṛṣṇa theme in the shrine.

(v) Aṣṭabhujagōpāla Shrine

In the shrine of Tondaradipoḍi Āḷvār, we find a stone image of Kṛṣṇa. It is actually dedicated to Kṛṣṇa with eight arms. The form is known as Madanagōpāla. We have an inscription of Nāyak period which registers gift of a village yielding a revenue of 600 *rekha-gadya* by one Chinna Bomma Nāyudu for worship and offerings to the image of Aṣṭabhuja Gopālakṛṣṇa built by him.[28]

(vi) Gōpālakṛṣṇa Shrine

The chief stone image in the sanctum of the Nāthamuni shrine is that of Gopālakṛṣṇa. It is a two-armed image in a *tribhanga* pose with the right hand holding a curved stick of a shepherd (*mannār*). Nearby, Balarāma is shown holding butter balls in both the hands.

An interesting inscription found in the south wall of the *prākāra* of Srīrangam temple dated in the 6th regnal year of the Chōḷa king Vīrarājēndradēva registers gift of the village Tiruvāypāḍinallūr, made tax-free for special worship and offerings to God, on the day of the Daivatharayan festival by the Gōpālas who had proprietary right over Valluvapāḍi-nāḍu.

(4) Pancha Kṛṣṇa Kshētras

We have already seen how after the Bhakti period the pilgrimage centres grew in number and the temple clusters began to be formed. One of such clusters is the *Pancha-Kṛṣṇa-Kshetras*—a cluster of five centres of worship. Of these four are in Chōḷanāḍu and one is in Nadu-nāḍu. They are Tirukaṇṇanguḍi, Tirukaṇṇapuram, Tirukaṇṇamangai, Kaṇṇan Kabistalam and Tirukōvalūr respectively. All these temples have been sung by the Āḷvārs. It is interesting to note that in North India also there are five sacred centres of Kṛṣṇa worship called Pancha-dvārakās.

An interesting feature that is common to all the five temples is that the iconic forms of all the presiding deities of these temples are not of Kṛṣṇa but only general Viṣṇu forms, with four arms holding *sankha*, *chakra*, *gadā* and the *abhaya* or *varada mudrā*. They cannot be called as a form of Kṛṣṇa. Then how did they get the name "Kṛṣṇa Kshetras"? As far as we know, the name must have been derived from the place names, the processional deities and the *sthalapurāṇas*. For instance, in Tirukaṇṇanguḍi, the *utsavamūrti* is called

Dāmodara Nārāyaṇa and the *Sthalapurāṇa* associates the place with Kṛṣṇa. According to the *Purāṇa*, Maharishi Vasiṣṭa was worshipping an image of Kṛṣṇa, made of butter. One day, the Lord himself came and ate the butter image. When Vasiṣṭa tried to catch him, Kṛṣṇa ran towards the sages who with their *bhakti* had already tied down Kṛṣṇa there.

Likewise, in Tirukōvalūr, though the presiding deity is Trivikrama, the *utsava-bēra* is called Āyanār, Kōvalan or Gōpālan. Another name for Tirukōvalūr is Kṛṣṇāraṇya-kshetra. There are separate shrines for Kṛṣṇa and his sister Durgā in the temple. In Kaṇṇan Kabistalam, the main deity is known as "reclining Kṛṣṇa on the river bank".

(5) Kṛṣṇa Temple, Kāvalambāḍi (Thanjavur District)

There are three temples exclusively for Kṛṣṇa in Tirunāngūr region, near Māyavaram, in Thanjavur district. The first of these temples is in Kāvalambādi. Kāvalam means 'elephant', denoting Kṛṣṇa's killing the elephant demon. Tirumangaiāḷvār refers to this.[29] The main stone image is Gōpālakṛṣṇa or Rājagōpāla in standing form with two consorts Rukmini and Satyabhāmā. The temple is very simple in style.

(6) Pārthan Paḷḷi (Thanjavur District)

Another temple is for Kṛṣṇa as Pārthasārathi. The place is called Pārthan Paḷḷi. The *utsava* image is named as Pārthasārathi. Both the *mūlava* and *utsava* images have three consorts namely Srīdēvi, Bhūdēvi and Nīlādēvi. Nīla is normally taken for Nappinnai, and she is given a place on par with other two *dēvis.* There is a separate shrine for Arjuna in this temple. According to the *Sthalapurāṇa,* the concluding verses of the *Gītā* were taught to Arjuna in this place. This is another instance of localisation of the myths.

(7) Arimēyaviṇṇagar, Tirunāngūr (Thanjavur District)

The temple is popularly known as *Kudamāḍumkūttār* temple. An interesting form of Kṛṣṇa has been set up as the main deity in this temple. The seated stone image of Kṛṣṇa is keeping his leg on a pot and the name of the deity is Kuḍamādunakūttan i.e. the pot dancer. Tirumangaiāḷvār in his verses addresses the deity of this temple as *Kudamāḍumkūttār* (Oh, the pot dancer!).[30]

(8) Āmaruviyappar Temple, Tiruvalundur (Thanjavur District)

One of the important Kṛṣṇa temples in the Chōḷamaṇḍalam is the one in Tiruvalundur or Tēralundar near Māyavaram. The main *mūlava* image is called Devādhirāja. The *utsava* image is known as Āmaruviyappan meaning 'one who grazed the cattle'. The metal image of Kṛṣṇa is two-armed with a whip in one hand, another arm placed on a cow. He is surrounded by cows and accompanied by his two consorts.

The two inscriptions from the temple of Kilaiyūr (Thanjavur) dated 15th and 17th years of Rājarāja I (1000-1002 A.D.) record setting up of the images of Kṛṣṇa and Goddess in the temple at Tiruvalundur.[31]

We also get some more inscriptions of the same period which mention the deity as Sri Kṛṣṇa and register the gifts made to the temple like lands and sheep. Another inscription registers the grants made for the provision of ghee or refined butter (*neyamuthu*) to the deity.

(9) Rājagōpālaswāmi Temple, Mannārkudi (Thanjavur District)

This is one of the foremost centres of Kṛṣṇa worship in Tamilnāḍu hailed as the Southern Dwārakā. The presiding deity is Vāsudēva Perumāḷ with his consorts. The processional deity is known as Rājagōpālaswāmin. He is flanked by Rukmini and Satyabhāmā on either side.

Six inscriptions found in the temple belong to the periods of Kulōttunga Chōḷa I, Rājarājadēva Chōḷa and Konerimaykōṇḍa. It is understood that this temple was built in the 43rd regnal year of Kulōttunga I (1113 A.D.) and the temple was known as Kulōttunga Chōḷa Viṇṇagaram. In one of the inscriptions dated in the year 1266 A.D. the names of the deity and his consort are mentioned as *Vantuvarāpati Mahāmunikal* and *Periyapirāṭṭi* respectively.[32] We learn from an inscription that the temple lands were not taxed by the king and that the revenue from the lands was utilised for the conduct of temple services and the celebration of festivals.[33]

According to the *sthalapurāṇa*, Kṛṣṇa showed his childhood sports to the sage Gopralaya Maharishi at this place and hence it is also known as *Dakshina Dwārakā* i.e. Dwārakā of the South. The annual Brahmotsava festival and boat festival are celebrated on a grand scale. The temple has been glorified by Āchārya Manavāla Māmunikal (15th century). *Vennai-Thāḷi* (butter pot) festival in particular is famous here and attracts huge crowds from all over Tamilnāḍu. Devotees offer butter in large quantities to the deity on the occasion. The term Rājagōpāla means 'the king of the cowherds'. This form of Kṛṣṇa was popularised in iconic form also during the Chōḷa period and we have a number of exquisite metal icons of Rājagōpāla with his consorts from many places as shown in Chapter V.

As we have seen, during the period of Chōḷas, the dancing form of Kṛṣṇa was placed in all Viṣṇu temples even as the dancing form of Siva (Naṭarāja) was placed in all Siva temples. We have an inscription of the time of Rājarāja I dated in 1008 A.D. from Kumbakonam, stating the gift of land for a lamp to the shrine of Veṇṇaikūttādi Aruḷuginra-Āḷvār (Kṛṣṇa) in Tirunārāyaṇa Vinnagar.[34] Rājarāja Chōḷa I donated silver idols of Vāsudēva to the Great Temple built by him at Thanjavur.

(10) Kṛṣṇa Temples at Thanjavur Palace

Five temples attached to the Devasthanam in Thanjavur palace are dedicated to Kṛṣṇa. They are:

(1) Navanīta Kṛṣṇa
(2) Bhūlōga Kṛṣṇa
(3) Mannārswāmi
(4) Madanagōpālaswāmi
(5) Vēnugōpālaswāmi.

All of them seem to have come up during the rule of the Nāyaks of Thanjavur and the Mahrattas from the 16th century onwards.

(11) Kudandai Navanītakṛṣṇa Temple (Kumbakōnam)

According to local tradition this temple was originally built for Periyāḷvār. When a separate chamber was made for the Āḷvārs in Sarangapani temple, the people of the locality consecrated the image of Navanīta Kṛṣṇa here and celebrated festivals. The *mūlabēra* is Venugōpāla and the *utsava* image is Navanīta-Kṛṣṇa.

Naḍu-Nāḍu

A part of the present South Arcot district was known as Naḍu-nāḍu. The most important shrine here being Tirukkōvalur, an ancient and holy place for the Vaiṣṇavas of Tamilnāḍu.

(1) Trivikrama Temple, Tirukkōvalūr (South Arcot District)

This temple actually is dedicated to Trivikrama form of Viṣṇu, but the place name (Kōvalūr) denotes its association with Kṛṣṇa. The processional deity of the temple is called Āyanār and Kōvalan (meaning shepherd). As already mentioned, this place is one of the *Pancha-Kṛṣṇa-kshētras.*

We get an inscription of Vijayanagar period, recording that the shrine of Kṛṣṇa and the Vaikuṇṭha-vāsal in the temple at Tirukkōvalūr were built by Acchutamman, daughter of Kṛṣṇappa Nāyak and that a village was endowed for providing worship to Kṛṣṇa. It clearly shows the royal patronage received by the cult during the Vijayanagar times. Another interesting inscription dated in the 14th year of the Chōḷa king Tribhuvana Chakravartin Rājarājadēva found in this temple refers to a land measure called *Vennaikūttan-kadi.*[35] The *uri-aḍi* festival on the occasion of Kṛṣṇa-Jayanti is a very popular festival here which attracts large crowds. The shepherd community takes a leading part in this festival.

(2) *Vēnugōpālaswāmin Temple, Sirumadurai (South Arcot District)*

There is another temple for Kṛṣṇa in the village called Sirumadurai near Tirukkoyilur, known as Vēnugōpālaswāmin temple. Though this temple is not sung by the Āḷvārs, we get some Pāṇḍya inscriptions, one of which records a gift of land to the temple. It is dated 1291 A.D. during the time of Vikrama Pāṇḍya.[36] The name of the village Sirumadurai which means "small Madurai" may also signify Kṛṣṇa's association with Mathura.

(3) *Kāṭṭumannār Kōil (South Arcot District)*

Another ancient centre of Kṛṣṇa worship in the modern South Arcot district is Kāṭṭumannār Kōil. The temple is known as Vīranārāyaṇaswāmin temple. There are shrines for Aḷagiya Mannār and Rājagōpālaswāmi.

Kāṭṭumannār Kōil was the birth place of the Vaiṣṇava preceptor Nāthamuni who codified 4000 hymns of the Āḷvārs.[37]

There are numerous inscriptions in the temple. The Kṛṣṇa shrines in the temple are referred to as Tuvarāpati-Emberumān (Lord of Dwārakā) temple[38] and Mathurapati-Emberumān (Lord of Mathura)[39] and the Lord as Mannanār in the inscriptions belonging to Kāḍavan and Pāṇḍya kings. The inscription of Pāṇḍya king Jatāvarman Sundara Pāṇḍya records the sale of house site by the trustees of the Mathurapati-Emberumān temple for constructing and maintaining a *maṭha* for feeding ascetics and Vaiṣṇavas therein.

(4) *Pārthasārathi Temple, Devapāndalam (South Arcot District)*

The origin of the temple is not known, though the *Sthalapurāṇa* claims a hoary antiquity. It is claimed that it was here that the sacred utensil known as *akshaya-pātra* was given to Draupadi by Lord Kṛṣṇa. The name could be the corrupt form of 'Pāṇḍuvanam'. The presiding deity is quite tall having a whip in his right hand.

Pāṇḍya-Nāḍu

It has already been mentioned in the first chapter how Kṛṣṇa was closely associated with the Pāṇḍya kings. Their capital city Madurai often mentioned as "Southern Mathura" was probably named after Mathura, the birth place of Kṛṣṇa.

Apart from Madurai, we have certain other Kṛṣṇa centres situated in Pāṇḍya country which comprises erstwhile Rāmanāthapuram, Tirunelveli and Madurai districts.[40] Among the 108 holy Vaiṣṇava temples, 18 are in Pāṇḍya country. Of these 18 temples, we have four or five places which were predominantly Kṛṣṇa-worship centres. Madurai and Tirumālirunsōlai are as old as the Sangam works. From the Sangam literature, we know that temples for Kṛṣṇa and Balarāma were situated in these places. Many Pāṇḍya kings were devotees of Kṛṣṇa and Balarāma and worshipped them at Irungunram (Tirumālirunsōlai). At present, the temple in Tirumālirunsōlai, also known as Alagarkōil, is dedicated to Viṣṇu as *Kal-aḷagar*. Many Āḷvārs have glorified this temple in their hymns. A very popular festival which draws thousands of people every year is conducted for him. He is taken in procession in a horse-mount to the banks of the Vaigai to meet his sister Mīnākshi the Goddess at Madurai.

(1) Madurai

Pāṇḍyan inscriptions make reference to the temple of Kariyamānikka Perumāḷ within the premises of the present Minakshi temple. This deity was probably Kṛṣṇa. There are also temples for Madanagōpāla and Santānagōpāla in Madurai. There is also a temple for Navanīta Kṛṣṇa though of late origin, but is presently popular in Madurai. These Kṛṣṇa temples are patronised particularly by the Yādava and Saurashtra communities besides the Vaiṣṇava Brahmins.

(2) Vīranārāyaṇa Temple, Tiruttangal

This is an ancient Vaiṣṇava centre. The temple is situated on a hillock. There are three tiers, each having a separate shrine, one above the other. The topmost shrine being the main one is dedicated to Kṛṣṇa and his family members. Along with Kṛṣṇa, images of his four consorts, namely, Rukmini, Satyabhāmā, Nīlādēvi and Jāmbavati, his son Pradyumna, and his grandson Aniruddha are placed inside the shrine. The temple dates from an early period as it had been sung by the Bhūdattāḷvār of the 7th century A.D. and Tirumangai in 8th century A.D. The inscriptions in the temple range in dates from the early Chōḷa period down to the 13th century. From one of the inscriptions we know that the sanctum and the mahāmaṇḍapa were rebuilt by a minister called Gurukula-tharaiyan, during the reign of Māravarman Sundara Pāṇḍya.[41] Another inscription[42] belonging to the 5th regnal year of the same king records the gift of land by two brothers namely Thiruvarangadevan and

Uyyakkondan for the recital of *Mahābhārata*, *Rāmāyaṇa* and the *Purāṇas* in front of the Lord of Thiruttankal. It is called *Mahābhārata-Virutti.*

According to the *Sthalapurāṇa*, this was where Aniruddha, the grandson of Kṛṣṇa, married Usha.

(3) Vatapatrasāyi Temple, Srivilliputtūr

The birth place of Periyāḷvār and Āṇḍāḷ is Srivilliputtūr in Virudhunagar district. The presiding deity of the temple Vaḍaperunkōil is Vatapatrasāyi or Rangamannār. Vatapatrasāyi is the name given to Kṛṣṇa lying on the leaf floating on the primordial ocean glorified by the Aḷvārs. This is the place where Āṇḍāḷ imagined herself as a gōpikā and observed the *Pāvai-nōnbu* ritual to win the Lord himself as her husband. This is the place where Periyāḷvār sang those scintillating songs on Kṛṣṇa's childhood.

There are many Pāṇḍyan and Nāyak inscriptions found in the temple. They provide us with some interesting details regarding the history of this temple. For instance, Tamil inscription of Saka 1375 (A.D. 1453) commences with a long preamble relating to the mythical connection between Lord Kṛṣṇa and Sūḍikkodutta Nācchiyār (i.e. Āṇḍāḷ) in this village.[43]

Another interesting inscription of Sundarapāṇḍyadēva records the deduction in the tax on the lands belonging to the temple.[44]

From an inscription of Saka 1493 (A.D. 1571) found in the Kṛṣṇa temple here, we know that the temple was built by Srivallabhadēva for the merit of Vīrappa Nāyak.[45] Another record of the same year registers the grant of exemption from taxes on the lands which had been endowed to the temple of Kṛṣṇa.[46] Yet another record of the Nāyak period registers a tax-free grant of land as Sarvamānya to certain washermen to settle down in the village and continue their services to the temple of Kṛṣṇa. All these illustrate the royal patronage extended to the temple.

(4) Ādinātha Perumāḷ Temple, Vijayanārāyaṇam (Tirunelveli Dt.)

In the Ādinātha Perumāḷ temple at Vijayanārāyaṇam in Nanguneri taluk of Tirunelveli district, a Pāṇḍyan inscription registers a gift of land by a woman devotee for the worship of Kṛṣṇa whose image she had set up in the temple of Varaguna-Viṇṇagar Emberumān.[47] Here Kṛṣṇa is referred to as Tiruvāykkuḷathu-Piḷḷai meaning "the boy of the cowherd clan". Another record gives the name of Kṛṣṇa as Yādava-nārāyaṇa.

An inscription in the shrine of Rājagōpālaswāmin in the temple belonging to Pāṇḍya ruler refers to some gift of land made by the assembly of

Vijayanārāyaṇa Chaturvēdimangalam, which met in the central courtyard of the temple, for the expenses of offerings and worship to the God Yādava-nārāyaṇa-viṇṇagar-emberumān.[48] The Lord of the temple is also referred to as Aḷagiya-mannanār in some inscriptions.[49]

(5) *Rājagōpālaswāmi Temple, Mannārkoil, Ambasamudram Taluk*

The Rājagōpālaswāmi Temple, Mannārkoil is a historical temple. During the Chōḷa period it was known by the name Rājēndra Chōḷa-Viṇṇagaram, after Rājēndra I. The main deity is called Vēdanārāyaṇa. The temple is stated to have been built by Rājasimha, the Chēra feudatory and named after their overlord Rājēndra I. This temple must have been a big establishment as there were many gardeners, drummers, potters, garland makers, torch bearers and *dēvaradiyārs* attached to this temple.[50] As many as nine inscriptions have come down to us from this temple.

(6) *Thuvarāpati Appan Temple, Chēramādēvi*

In the same Ambasamudram taluk we get inscriptional reference to a temple called Appan temple at Chēramādēvi. An inscription of Vīra Pāṇḍya registers gifts made to the deity Thuvarāpati Appan (Lord of Dwārakā) for celebrating yearly festivals.[51] The temple was obviously for Kṛṣṇa. A beautiful bronze image of Kṛṣṇa in the Kaliyamardana form has come from this place (see Chapter V).

(7) *Vikramasingapuram, Ambasamudram Taluk*

This is a place very near Ambasamudram in Tirunelveli district. There is an old temple for Kṛṣṇa here noted for the celebration of Kṛṣṇa-Jayanti festival on a grand scale.

(8) *Aḷagiya Mannār Rājagōpālaswāmin Temple, Palayankottai (Tirunelveli Dt.)*

The huge temple was known as Champakāraṇya Kshetra according to the *Sthalapurāṇa.* The legend goes like this: The temple was patronised by Pāṇḍya chieftains of Manapadaivīdu. According to the temple legend a Pāṇḍyan chief Srī Bali is said to have constructed the main shrine for Vēdanārāyaṇa, the *ardha-maṇḍapa,* the *maṇi-maṇḍapa* and the flag-staff and celebrated festivals. The chief prayed to Vēdanārāyaṇa for a child and he was directed by the Lord to bring the images of Rājagōpāla and Rukmini lying under the river Gangā. The chief is said to have brought the images and consecrated them in the temple and he was blessed with a child.

The temple has a three-tier *vimāna.* On the topmost tier, we see the huge image of Rājagōpāla standing with his consorts, Srīdēvi and Bhūdevi. These images are made of stucco. On the walls of this shrine beautiful paintings can be seen. It was renovated in 1953.

Inside the main shrine, downstairs, the metal images of Rājagōpāla with his consorts Rukmini and Satyabhāmā are kept. The form of Kṛṣṇa is two-armed, the right arm holding a stick to graze the cattle and the left arm is resting on a cow. This is in line with the image of Rājagōpāla of Mannārkudi. Annual Srī-Jayanti festival is celebrated, besides other festivals. The temple must have been patronised by the Yādava community of the locality, who form a sizable part of the population of the place, even today.

(9) Nava-Tirupatis (Tirunelveli Dt.)

There is a cluster of nine holy Vaiṣṇava shrines renowned as *nava-tirupatis* which include the Āḷvār-tirunagari, the birth place of Nammāḷvār, Tirukkoilur, the birth place of Madurakavi Āḷvār and other well-known places like Srivaikuntam, Perunkulam etc. They have been sung by Nammāḷvār. In all the nine temples Kṛṣṇa is installed within the sanctum or in a separate shrine indicating the importance given to Kṛṣṇa. The presiding deity of Perunkulam is Kṛṣṇa as Māyakūthan. The sculptural work at Āḷvār Tirunagari is dominated by Kṛṣṇa theme. Sri Jayanti and Uriaḍi festivals, special for Kṛṣṇa, are popular in these temples.

(10) Dwārakā Kṛṣṇa Temple, Suchindram (Kanyakumari Dt.)

The temple is referred to as Dwaraka Emberuman temple in inscriptions dated A.D. 1227, 1228 and 1229.[52] The first inscription found in the central shrine of the temple records endowment of land by the *sabha* of Suchindram assembled at the *Tirucchutru-mandapa* in the temple of Suchindramuḍaiya Nāyanār for maintaining a perpetual lamp.

Another inscription records gift of 4 *vēlis* of land, for the daily services of the Dwarakai-Viṣṇubhagavān temple by one Kēsavan Arangan. Another inscription dated in 1228 A.D. refers to the digging of a tank named after Kṛṣṇa *Kaṇṇan-kuḷam.*[53]

(11) Kariyamāṇikkapuram (Kanyakumari Dt.)

The very name Kariyamāṇikkam, the "black gem", denotes Kṛṣṇa. We get a few inscriptions from this temple. From one of them dated in 1437 A.D., we know that the temple was renovated along with the *mahāmaṇḍapa* by one Kulasekara Nambirāṭṭiyār. The inscription dated 1509 A.D. refers to a donation to Kariyamāṇikka Viṇṇagar Perumāḷ for daily worship and also for the Sri-Jayanti festival.[54]

(12) Thōvalai (Kanyakumari Dt.)

This is very near Aralvoymoḷi the stronghold of the Āy Vēlir chieftains who claim descent from Kṛṣṇa. There is a temple for Kṛṣṇa where the Nambudris are the priests. Hence the temple rituals according to the Kerala tradition are followed here.

Kongu-Nāḍu

There are also many temples for Kṛṣṇa in the Kongu area, comprising the modern districts of Coimbatore, Salem, Erode, and Dharmapuri. But the inscriptional evidence is rather meagre. Temples for Vēnugōpāla are found at Erode, Coimbatore and Satyamangalam and they appear to belong to the Vijayanagar period. An inscription of Parāntaka Chōḷa I (10th century) from Madiraikonda (Coimbatore Dt.) mentions an endowment for the worship of Kṛṣṇa as Veṇṇaikūthanainār in the Viṣṇu temple at Erode.

Conclusion

Thus from the foregoing survey it can be seen that the temples of Kṛṣṇa were fairly widespread in Tamilnāḍu in the ancient and medieval times. It should be mentioned that apart from the fifty and odd temples with ancient inscriptions exclusively devoted to Kṛṣṇa as detailed above, almost every Viṣṇu temple in Tamilnāḍu has the consecrated metal image of Kṛṣṇa in some form or the other. As pointed out earlier, the image of Kṛṣṇa as a dancer with a butter ball (Navanīta Kṛṣṇa or Veṇṇai kūttan) was introduced in the Viṣṇu temples of Toṇḍaimaṇḍalam sometime during the Chōḷa period. In some temples especially from Vijayanagar times we find the image of Vēnugōpāla. This practice is also found in the temples of the Pāṇḍya region. In the Viṣṇu temples of Chōḷa-nāḍu the metal icon of Santāna-gōpāla (reclining child Kṛṣṇa) is very common. The practice of women devotees fondling the icon is in vogue and it is believed that they would be blessed with beautiful and intelligent child like Kṛṣṇa.

The foregoing survey also reveals that many towns and villages had separate quarters for the cowherd community often called Āypāḍi or Āykuḍi. In some inscriptions it is called Tiruvāypāḍi which also occurs in Tamil literature as equivalent of Gokulam (near Mathura in the north) where Kṛṣṇa grew up. It is interesting to note that in many Tamil inscriptions cited above, he is referred to as Tiruvāypāḍidēvar (the Lord of Gokula). We also get several instances of the patronage extended to Kṛṣṇa temples by the shepherd class (*manrādis* or *kōnars*). In one inscription, they are significantly called Nandaputras (Kṛṣṇa was also Nandakumāra) and Tiruvāypāḍi Nattar of Tondaimandalam and they met in the Kṛṣṇa temple at Tiruvattiyur on one occasion and expressed their gratitude to Kṛṣṇa for the divine grace bestowed on the community.[55]

The survey has also furnished good evidence of the association of other communities—the Brahmins, especially the Vaiṣṇavas, the Vellāla agriculturists, the merchants besides kings, queens and royal officers. So, Kṛṣṇa worship was fostered by all the communities of Tamilnāḍu, as it is done even today.

Another noteworthy point that emerges from the above survey is the several endearing Tamil names by which Kṛṣṇa was deified in the temples. The following examples can be cited:

Tirukkuḷal-ūdina-piḷḷai—the child who plays on the divine flute

Tiruvāypāḍi-Dēvār—Lord of Gokulam

Vennaikūttan—dancing with the butter ball

Āmaruviappan—one who grazed the cattle

Aḷagiya-mannār—the beautiful shepherd boy

Rājamannār—King of cowherds

Karaiamāṇikkam—the black gem

Tuvarāpati Appar—the Lord of Dwārakā

Mathurāpuri Emberumān—the Lord of Mathura

Brindāvana Emberumān—the Lord of Brindāvan

Kurukshetra-deva—the Lord or Hero of Kurukshetra

An interesting feature reflected in the names of the temples and places is the process of the localisation of Kṛṣṇa in Tamilnāḍu. Mannārkuḍi in Thanjavur district which has a famous temple for Kṛṣṇa as Rājagōpāla is called the Dwārakā of the south. Tiruvallikeni (in Chennai city) where there is an ancient temple for Pārthasārathi, is regarded by the Vaiṣṇavas as the Brindāvan of the south.

The inscriptions discussed above also reveal that endowments were made by several sections of the society for celebrating festivals in honour of Kṛṣṇa such as his birthday (Kṛṣṇa Jayanti) and *Uri-aḍi*[56] and also recitation of the Āḷvārs' hymns in praise of Kṛṣṇa like *Tiruppāvai, Tiruvāymoḷi*. Thus, the study of the inscriptions and the tradition of Kṛṣṇa temples of Tamilnāḍu clearly reflect how Kṛṣṇa worship, with its deep roots in the Sangam and the Bhakti and post-Bhakti religious literature was integrated with the temple culture of Tamilnāḍu.

References

1. Rama Rao, M., *Temples of Tirumalai and Tirupati*, p. 47.
2. 239 of 1903. Another inscription dated A.D. 1564 mentions the five deities Kṛṣṇa, Rukmini, Baladēva, Madana, Aniruddha and Sātyaki.
3. *ARE* No. 641 of 1919.
4. Raman, K.V., *Sri Varadarajaswami Temple, Kanchi.*

4a. D. Hudson, *Srimad Bhagavata Purana in Stone, Journal of Vaisnava Studies*, Vol. 3, No. 3, 1995.

5. *ARE* No. 2 of 1892.
6. *ARE* No. 29 of 1896.
7. *ARE* No. 26 of 1896. The Āḷvārs frequently address Kṛṣṇa as *Vantuvarāpati mannan* (King of Dwaraka) *Nammāḷvār* 5-3-6.
8. 3 of 1892.
9. 283 to 292 of 1897.
10. 292 of 1897.
11. 291 of 1897.
12. Francois Gros and R. Nagaswamy, *Uttaramerur: Legends, History and Monuments*, Pondicherry, 1970.
13. *Ibid.*
14. 187 of 1923.
15. 292 of 1897.
16. 167 of 1915.
17. 312 of 1906.
18. 333 of 1906.
19. 246 of 1909.
20. 71 of 1887; 456-472 of 1925, 274 to 283 of 1953-54.
21. 273 of 1977-78.
22. 330 of 1917.
23. 540 of 1905-06.
24. 534 of 1905.
25. Aravamuthan, T.G., *Transactions of the Archaeological Society of South India*, 1962-65, pp. 63-67.
26. 69 of 1936-37.
27. 74 of 1892. He was probably the Naik Chieftain of Vellore.
28. 102 of 1937-38.

29. *Periya Tirumoḷi,* 4-6-8.
30. *Ibid.,* 3-10-8.
31. 91 and 93 of 1925.
32. 105 of 1897.
33. 102 of 1897.
34. 326 of 1910.
35. 339 of 1921.
36. 268 of 1936-37.
37. Vide Chapter III.
38. 534 of 1920; *SII,* Vol.12, 254.
39. 529 of 1920.
40. Recently the three old districts have been re-organised into many smaller units.
41. 554 of 1922.
42. 546 of 1922.
43. 577 of 1926.
44. 541 of 1926.
45. 591 of 1926.
46. 592 of 1926.
47. 18 of 1927.
48. 20 of 1927.
49. 23 and 25 of 1927.
50. 107 of 1905; *SII,* Vol. XIV, No. 132. Tirumalai, R., *Rājēndra Chōḷa Viṇṇagaram.*
51. 185 of 1895.
52. *TAS,* VIII, pp. 37-38.
53. *Ibid.,* p. 36.
54. *Kanyakumari Kalvettukkal.*
55. See No. 18 above under Toṇḍai-nāḍu.
56. A mock contest performed by the shepherds to get the prize money kept at the top of a tall pole smeared with oil. One who successfully went up the pole could get the prize money.

Chapter V

KṚṢṆA THEME IN THE ART OF TAMILNĀḌU

Introduction

The deep impact that Kṛṣṇa's life and teachings made on the poets, saints and scholars and religious leaders of Tamilnāḍu also inspired the Tamil artists—the sculptors, the metal icon makers, the painters, the wood and ivory carvers—through many centuries. Tamil artists of every generation have revelled in giving expression to some new form of Kṛṣṇa in stone, metal or wood. Regarding the stone sculpture, the earliest sculptors of Tamilnāḍu, belonging to the Pallava period, have handled the Kṛṣṇa theme in a superb manner as can be seen at Māmallapuram, Kānchi, Tiruvellarai and other places. This period coincides with the Bhakti movement of the Vaiṣṇava saints Āḷvārs. In the Chōḷa period, we see the stone and metal sculptors vying with one another in giving expression to complex or difficult themes and expressions. Bold experimentation was made in metal casting and we have some masterpieces of bronze icons depicting Kṛṣṇa as the Kāḷiyā Kṛṣṇa, Bālakṛṣṇa, Navanīta Kṛṣṇa, Santānagōpāla, Rājagōpāla, Vēṇugōpāla, Pārthasārathi, coming from different parts of Tamilnāḍu, the like of which cannot be seen anywhere in India either quantitatively or qualitatively. Many of them display unique conception, powerful modelling and graceful execution. There are hundreds of Kṛṣṇa images in stone and metal belonging to the Chōḷa/Pāṇḍya periods (from 900 to 1300 A.D.) displaying variety in themes and style. Some of the outstanding ones are illustrated and discussed here. This large output was partly to meet the demands of the expansion of temple building activities of the Chōḷa times and partly to counter the competition that Vaiṣṇavism had to face from Saivism. We have interesting parallels in the metal icons of this period like the dancing Kṛṣṇa and dancing Siva (Naṭarāja); Kṛṣṇa leaning on the cow (Rājagōpāla) and Siva leaning on the bull (Vrishabhāntika); Kṛṣṇa playing on the flute (Muraḷīdhara) and Siva playing on the Vīṇā (Vīṇādhara). It was the Chōḷa artists who have given us the finest metal icons of the Kṛṣṇa and Siva themes. In general, the art critics and connoisseurs like Douglas Barrett and C. Sivaramamurti consider the Chōḷa metal icons of the 10th and 11th centuries as the finest ones, characterised by natural and flowing rhythm and innate originality. The same qualities can be seen in the metal images of Kṛṣṇa of this period, as will be shown in the sequel. A certain amount of conventionalism or standardisation of the images is however noticeable in the later Chōḷa times, but still they continue to hold our attention by their poise and grace.

The period roughly from 1300 A.D. to 1400 A.D. was a period of political confusion and cultural disturbance in South India due to various reasons like the fall of the major kingdoms like the Chōḷa and the Pāṇḍya and also the Muslim invasions (like those of Malik Kafur in 1310 A.D.). These had their adverse effects on the architectural and sculptural activities. But soon this period of lull was broken, and with the appearance of the new kingdom of Vijayanagar by the middle of the 14th century, temple art and culture received a fresh lease of life and it is reflected in the art productions of the period.

During this period of cultural resurgence, lavish patronage was extended to the temple building and sculptural activities. Not only were new temples built but the old ones were beautified by the addition of new *maṇḍapas* like the Kalyāṇa-maṇḍapa, Ūnjal-maṇḍapa, Vāhana-maṇḍapa etc. the pillars of which were profusely carved with sculptures, depicting the *Rāmāyaṇa*, the *Mahābhārata* and the *Purāṇic* themes. They can be seen in the leading temples of Tamilnāḍu like Sri Varadarājaswāmi Temple, Kānchi, Jalakantēsvara Temple, Vellore, Ranganātha Temple, Srīrangam, Pārthasārathi Temple, Triplicane and Ādikēsava Temple at Sriperumbudur. In the sculptures of the Vijayanagar times, we notice greater prominence given to the Vaiṣṇava themes, especially Rāma and Kṛṣṇa. We have some of the best narrative panels of the *Rāmāyaṇa* and the Kṛṣṇa stories in sculptures and paintings of this period from places like Humpi, Lepakshi, Tirumalai, Tirupati, Kānchi, Tiruvannāmalai and Srirangam. Apart from depicting episodes in the narrative panels, we also notice some new and exaggerated forms of Kṛṣṇa executed like chaturbhuja and aṣṭabhuja-Vēṇugōpāla and Madanagōpāla.[1] Many shrines for Vēṇugōpāla appeared during this time. It was also during this period that the cult of Kṛṣṇa as Pāṇḍuranga or Viṭṭaladēva was introduced in Tamilnāḍu. This form which was popular in Maharashtra centring round Paṇḍaripura was popularised by the Vijayanagar kings like Krishnadēvarāya. A magnificent temple for Viṭṭala was built at Humpi, the capital of the Vijayanagar kingdom. It also spread to Tamilnāḍu and we see shrines for Viṭṭala in places like Srirangam and Viṭṭalapuram in Tirunelveli district.

Two other important developments during the Vijayanagar and Nāyak periods were the appearance of exquisite paintings and wood works depicting among other themes the *Bhāgavatapurāṇa*. Paintings with Kṛṣṇa theme are to be seen in many temples of Tamilnāḍu and the Vijayanagar influence is clearly attested by the Telugu label inscriptions found on them. They are seen in places like Kānchi (Jaina temples at Jaina-Kānchi[2] and also the Varadarāja temple at Vishnu-Kānchi), Srirangam,[3] Tiruvellarai, Ādamankottai (Dharmapuri Dt.) and Alagarkōil (Madurai Dt.).

This was also the period when a number of wooden cars or chariots were made and donated to the temples. These cars are veritable temples on wheels and meant for processions. They carry some exquisite wood carvings of *purāṇic* stories. We see in temple cars at Kānchi, Srirangam, Srivilliputtūr and Mannārgudi some good examples of wood carvings of Kṛṣṇa theme. We also have some rare specimens of ivory carvings in Srirangam temple. All these are discussed in greater detail in this chapter.

Early Specimens

As already pointed out, Kṛṣṇa worship was fairly popular in Tamilnāḍu even in the Sangam age but no monumental or iconic specimens have come down to us. The earliest available sculptural representations of Kṛṣṇa belong to the Pallava times. They are to be found in places like Māmallapuram, Kānchi, Tiruvellarai and Kavēripākkam. The most impressive of the early sculptures is that of Kṛṣṇa as Gōvardhanadhāri found as a gigantic relief sculpture at Māmallapuram datable to the second half of the 7th century A.D. (Fig. 4). This is found very close to the famous Arjuna's penance sculptural-panel and has been rightly ascribed to the same period.[4] Here, the Pallava artists have achieved a remarkable feat of putting the two episodes from two major purāṇic themes in the plastic form—Arjuna's penance from the *Mahābhārata* and Gōvardhanadhāri Kṛṣṇa from the *Viṣṇu Purāṇa.* In both the cases, they have succeeded in presenting a powerful visual impact on the onlooker. Both the panels arrest our attention not only by their vast size but also by the dexterous grouping of the characters, variety of forms and graceful depiction. Here, Kṛṣṇa stands as a central figure, a virtual hero, effortlessly lifting the mighty Gōvardhana hill to afford shelter and protection to the cowherds who crowd around him with their children and family. Close to him stands his inseparable brother Balarāma on one side, embracing a shepherd, and on the other, stands his favourite shepherd girl Nappinnai. The pastoral scene has been depicted in its simple and natural beauty. One lady is seen carrying a pile of pots in her hand and a rolled bed on her head (Fig. 5). Another shepherd is seen milking the cow while the cow is seen licking her calf. Yet another boy is seen playing on the flute much to the delight of the cows and men. The idea that under the protective care of Kṛṣṇa, there was nothing for them to fear and Indra's threat need not cause any panic and that they could attend to their normal daily chores, is powerfully brought out in the panel. The rural and the forest surroundings have been ably portrayed by showing the forest animals, here and there. It is no wonder that art-historians have regarded this panel as one of the great masterpieces of not only Pallava but indeed the Indian art as a whole.[5]

Another sculpture of Kṛṣṇa is to be found in the Dharmarāja-ratha at Māmallapuram.[6] It is a smaller relief sculpture showing Kṛṣṇa in the Kāliyamardana pose. It is found in one of the panels on the middle tier of the roof in the Dharmarāja-ratha. Here two-armed Kṛṣṇa is trampling Kāliya, represented by a human torso with a serpent tail and three-headed serpenthood. He has his left foot on Kāliya's nape. He holds the tail with his arms (Fig. 6).

Vaikuṇṭaperumāḷ Temple, Kānchi

Next in point of time are the sculptures of Kṛṣṇa theme found in Vaikuṇṭaperumāḷ temple, Kānchi built by Nandivarman II in 8th century A.D. The temple is dedicated to Viṣṇu in three forms—seated, standing and reclining—found in shrines on the ground, the first and the second floor respectively. There are a number of sculptural relief panels on the sanctum walls and the niches representing Viṣṇu in different forms and themes. One of them is a large panel of Nara and Nārāyaṇa, a conceptual representation of Arjuna and Kṛṣṇa, the latter in the *vyākhyāna-mudrā*, teaching his disciple. This sculpture recalls a similar one found at the famous Gupta temple of Dasavatara at Deogarh. A sculpture of Kāliyamardana is also found in relief on the second floor, but it is badly weathered and worn out. Dennis Hudson who has made a detailed study of this temple describes it as the "Bhagavata Purana in stone". The fifty-six sculptural panels on the *vimāna*, with a few exceptions, are those of the *BGP.* Kṛṣṇa theme dominates. Among them are: Kṛṣṇa teaching Uddhava, Kṛṣṇa and Balarāma in Akrura's chariot, killing of Kesi, Dantavaktra, Sisupāla, Kamsa, etc.[6a]

Pundarikāksha Temple, Tiruvellarai, Tiruchi District

This is an exquisite Pallava temple dedicated to Viṣṇu and situated on the banks of the Kāveri almost on the southern frontiers of the Pallava territory. It was built by Dantivarman Pallava (796-847 A.D.), who was an ardent patron of Vaiṣṇavism. As pointed out earlier, this was a temple dedicated to Kṛṣṇa and Rukmini as borne out by the inscription of Dantivarman. We get a number of exquisite little sculptures depicting Kṛṣṇa and his various sports, on the walls of the *vimāna* base and the *swastika* shaped temple tank. The most interesting among them is the one which shows Kṛṣṇa as a pot-dancer or *Kuḍakkūttu.* Reference to this form of Kṛṣṇa is found in the Sangam literature and in the works of the Āḷvārs. Here is a beautiful sculptural representation of this unique theme (Fig. 7). Kṛṣṇa is seen dancing in the *swastika* (cross-legged) pose effortlessly playing the pot on one of his shoulders. He is depicted with his typical bun-like hair-do (*kēsa-bandha*) and bedecked with ornaments like the *patra-kuṇḍalas*, a heavy *hāra, yajnōpavita, udarabandha, kaṭibandha, bhujanga-vaḷaya, kankaṇas* and *nūpuru* (anklet). The dance movement is brought out excellently in this sculpture. This is one of the very few sculptures depicting Kṛṣṇa in this theme. Another interesting episode from Kṛṣṇa's childhood, *Bakāsuravadha*, is also depicted in a sculpture. Here, Kṛṣṇa keeps the leg on the bird-like demon and kills him by tearing the bird's bill (Fig. 8).

There are quite a few other sculptures depicting Kṛṣṇa in other forms like Kāliya-mardana and Gōvardhanadhāri in the same temple.

Kāvēripākkam

Among the ruins of the temples of Kāvēripākkam (North Arcot district) now preserved in the Government Museum, Chennai, are the two exquisite, low relief figures of Kṛṣṇa. They are found in the *kūdu* arches of the temples. One is Kṛṣṇa as Venugōpāla and the other in the Kāliyamardana pose (Figs. 9 and 10). In the former, Kṛṣṇa is surrounded by cows and birds which crowd around him to hear his music. The practice of depicting miniature Kṛṣṇa forms in *kūdu* arches can be seen in late Pallava or early Chōḷa temples. This Kāvēripākkam temple is ascribed to Pallava-Chōḷa transition period of 9th century A.D.

Since the specimens of the Pallava times are limited and unique, they have been discussed in a separate section above. But as the temples and sculptures of Kṛṣṇa began to increase steadily during the Chōḷa, Pāṇḍya, Vijayanagar and Nāyak periods, it is more convenient to trace the art forms of Kṛṣṇa thematically and at the same time follow a chronological order as far as possible. In this order, we have the advantage of seeing the continuity as well as the change that had occurred in the treatment of the subject. We can observe how in the treatment of the same subject, the artists of the different periods have shown their ingenuity, as well as the regional traditions and idioms in which they were steeped. We cannot fail to notice the simple and natural forms of the Pallava or Chōḷa period, in contrast to the exuberant and somewhat conventional forms shown in the Vijayanagar and Nāyak times.

Our perspective in this discussion is not only to show the wide range of themes handled, but also the variations in the forms and styles that came into vogue from time to time. One of the important characteristics of Indian art is that while there is unity in the main theme there is infinite variety in the forms, depending upon the regional art-styles and local traditions. This can be truly seen with regard to Kṛṣṇa theme in the following pages. For instance, the iconographic conceptions of Kṛṣṇa-Nappinnai combination, Santāna Kṛṣṇa, Vēnkaṭakṛṣṇa combination with the Lord of Venkatam, Kṛṣṇa as Rājamannār are some of the unique contributions of Tamilnāḍu. Another important point worthy of special notice by the art-historians, is that it is Tamilnāḍu which has produced the largest number of bronze images of Kṛṣṇa, known for their vast range in themes and high artistic quality. If North India has given us a vast collection of paintings of Kṛṣṇa theme represented by the several schools like Rajput, Mughal, Pahari, Kangra etc. it is Tamilnāḍu which abounds in Kṛṣṇa bronzes of exquisite beauty and elegance belonging to different schools, Chōḷa, Pāṇḍya, Vijayanagar and Nāyak. Perhaps nowhere else do we get such an array of bronzes which can be placed in an unbroken chain of continuity from the 10th to 18th centuries. It clearly indicates how strong and vibrant was Kṛṣṇa worship here which alone could have provided the necessity of making the processional deities. This continuity matches well with the continuous flow of Tamil and Sanskrit literature on Kṛṣṇa that we discussed in the previous chapters.

(1) Bālakṛṣṇa or Vaṭapatrasāyi Kṛṣṇa

As a charming child, he has been a favourite theme of the poets as well as the artists. One of the recurring themes of the early Chōḷa temples is Kṛṣṇa as Vaṭapatrasāyi i.e. child Kṛṣṇa reclining on banyan leaf, sucking his toe held in one hand. This is found usually in the sculptural freeze on the *prastara* (entablature) of the early Chōḷa temples, both Saiva and Vaiṣṇava. Temples of Tennēri, Tirusulam are typical examples for such representation. In this form, Kṛṣṇa is conceived as an eternal Godhead who floats on the primordial flood. The photograph included here is the relief sculpture found on a pillar in the Jalakantēsvara temple at Vellore belonging to Vijayanagar period of 16th century (Fig. 11).

(2) Yasōdā-Kṛṣṇa

Yasōdā, the mother is shown suckling her child Kṛṣṇa in two beautiful bronze images of the Chōḷa period (11th century, Figs. 12 and 13). Though they are from different places they show almost identical details. Yasōdā beautifully dressed and seated on a pedestal with her left hand leaning on the seat and her right hand holding up the head of the child lying on her lap for breast feeding. The large *patrakuṇḍalas* in her ears and other ornaments are noteworthy.

(3) Crawling Kṛṣṇa

Another favourite child form is crawling Kṛṣṇa, usually with a butter ball and sometimes without it. A number of bronze images of crawling Kṛṣṇa belonging to Chōḷa and Vijayanagar times have come down to us. Recently, in the excavations done in the premises of the famous Chōḷa temple at Dārasuram, an exquisite bronze image of Kṛṣṇa was discovered. It belongs to 11th century A.D. (Fig. 14). Similar bronze images have also come to light from Naykanaipperiyal, in Tiruchi Dt. (Fig. 15). Another bronze image of crawling Kṛṣṇa found at Ulundangudi, Tiruchi Dt. belongs to 16th century. It is also listed here to show the later style (Fig. 16). The practice of offering metal or wooden figures of crawling Kṛṣṇa as votive offerings is popular in many temples of South India.

(4) Santāna-Gōpāla

This form was particularly popular in Thanjavur district during the Chōḷa period. Almost in every Vaiṣṇava temple it is found in the sanctum. Women devotees without children offer special worship to Kṛṣṇa. The bronze figure is given to them to be fondled for some time, and by this it is believed that they will have progeny (*santāna*). Usually, the image of Santāna-Gōpāla is placed on a Nāga seat. Kṛṣṇa is shown sucking his toe. A typical one from Karaikovilapattu is illustrated here (Fig. 17). Sometimes, the image of Santāna Kṛṣṇa is also shown without a nāga (Fig. 18). The practice of donating small wooden toy cradles for Santāna Kṛṣṇa by ladies who desire to have child is in vogue in many temples.

(5) Kṛṣṇa Killing Demons

Kṛṣṇa's boyhood sports were of great fascination to the Tamil artists as much as they were for the Tamil poets. They never felt tired of portraying Kṛṣṇa in his mischievous postures. His encounters with various demons like Bakāsura, and his victory over the serpent demon, Kāliya and the elephant demon Kuvalayāpiṭa are all well treated by the sculptors of Tamilnāḍu. A series of stone sculptures of the later Chōḷa period in Thiruvendipuram temple near Cuddalore depict the above episodes. One of them shows Kṛṣṇa in the act of plucking the tusk of the elephant, Kuvalayāpita (Fig. 19). A sculpture of Bakāsura-vadha is also found (Fig. 20). Another beautiful sculpture of Kṛṣṇa's Bakāsura-vadha is in the Ādikēsava temple, Sriperumbudur near Chennai (Fig. 21). Here, Kṛṣṇa is shown tearing the bill of the crane into two. A sculpture depicting Bakāsura-vadha in Varadarājaswāmi temple, Kānchi is a noteworthy piece (Fig. 22). Both Figures 21 and 22 are of the Vijayanagar period (16th century).

There is a beautiful sculpture in Varadarājaswāmi temple, at Kānchi, showing Kṛṣṇa as Gōvardhanagiridhāri. Here, he is shown with four arms, two bearing the *sankha* and the *chakra*, another right arm lifting the mountain. The noteworthy point in this piece is that Indra is shown with his elephant, worshipping Kṛṣṇa (Fig. 23). In the Gōvardhana panel at Mahābalipuram of Pallava period Kṛṣṇa is shown only with two arms. But during Vijayanagar period Kṛṣṇa was often depicted with more than two arms to show his supremacy as God.

(6) Kṛṣṇa as Navanīta-Chōra (Butter thief)

Another enchanting theme for the poets as well as the artists was Kṛṣṇa as a butter thief. His liking for it and in the process getting beaten for it are widely sung by the Āḻvārs and other poets. In the same way, the artists treat the theme in the sculptural medium too with great relish.

Among the series of Kṛṣṇa sculptures in Thiruvendipuram, one shows Kṛṣṇa gulping the butter from a pot hanging above (Fig. 24). The hanging-pot is called *uri* in Tamil. Kṛṣṇa with the help of his friends climbs up and reaches the pot and distributes the butter freely to his friends. It is beautifully portrayed in many sculptures. Two examples are given here (Figs. 25 and 26) from Kānchipuram and Thirukkurungudi respectively. Sometimes, Kṛṣṇa is joined by his brother Balarāma and both deceive their mother Yasōdā and get away with the butter (Fig. 27). This beautiful sculpture from Virunjipuram shows Kṛṣṇa taking out the butter from the pot right in front of Yasōdā while Balarāma is closing her eyes from behind. Kṛṣṇa is also shown caught by his mother and punished. Yasōdā once bound him to a stone mortar for stealing butter which gave him the name Dāmōdara. This episode is often mentioned by the Āḻvārs. Here is a sculptural representation of the same episode from Kānchipuram (Fig. 28). Once caught red handed, he was punished. He was asked to hold his ears with his hands and made to do the exercise of standing and sitting alternately until he was asked to stop (Fig. 29).

(7) Navanīta-Kṛṣṇa

Bronze images of Kṛṣṇa with butter balls in either of his hands are quite many. Kṛṣṇa invariably is shown as a child with a plump belly decorated with rich ornaments like *arainān* (hip-band) and *golusu* (the anklet). Here, two illustrations are given to show the typical form of Navanīta Kṛṣṇa from the Navanita Kṛṣṇa Temple of Seramadēvi (Fig. 30) and Vēṇugōpālaswāmi temple, Satyamangalam respectively (Fig. 31).

Another interesting stone sculpture of Kṛṣṇa can be seen on a pillar in the Kilimaṇḍapa of Madurai Meenakshi temple. It shows Kṛṣṇa as a young boy with a butter ball in his left hand and a sugarcane in his right (Fig. 32)—a form of Madanagōpāla.

(8) Navanīta Nritta-Kṛṣṇa (Kṛṣṇa dancing with butter)

Kṛṣṇa is also depicted as a dancer with one leg lifted up and a butter ball in one of his hands. Here a bronze sculpture from Tirupuvanam in Thanjavur district shows a typical one of the above form. His left arm is stretched out while his right arm is holding a butter ball (Fig. 33).

There is a separate shrine for Navanītanardhana Kṛṣṇa in Ranganātha temple in Paḷḷikoṇḍa (Vellore district). Here, both the *mūlava* and *utsava* images are similar, having butter balls in both the hands, the left hand is stretched out, and his right leg is placed on a curd-churner. The images can be ascribed to the Vijayanagar times (Figs. 34 and 35).

(9) Nardhana Kṛṣṇa

Many beautiful dancing images of Kṛṣṇa are available showing the popularity of Kṛṣṇa as a dancer. Here, we must recollect that the old Tamil text *Silappadikāram* mentions various dance forms performed by Kṛṣṇa as a boy and as a youth. The Āḷvārs address him as *māyakūthan*, divine dancer. Here, five exquisite sculptures of dancing Kṛṣṇa are taken for our study. Each one is different from the other. Superficially, they all look alike, but a careful study reveals many subtle variations introduced by the artists.

The first bronze sculpture in our list is an exquisite Pāṇḍyan piece, which belongs to 10th-11th centuries. It is from Uttarakōsamangai and depicts the youthful Kṛṣṇa stretching out his left arm and showing his right arm in *abhaya-mudrā*. This dance-pose is called *chatura-tāṇḍava* as the legs form a square (*chatura*) with his right foot slightly lifted up (Fig. 36).

Another late Chōḷa bronze depicting Kṛṣṇa as a dancer is also taken up for our study (Fig. 37). Kṛṣṇa is decorated with many beautiful ornaments like the crown, earrings, necklaces, shoulder bands, hip belts and anklets. Placing his slightly bent left leg down, he is raising his right leg. His left arm stretches out in the familiar form, but his right arm is seen in *sūchi-hasta* pose i.e. with a finger pointing towards something.

Another noteworthy bronze image of Kṛṣṇa has come down to us from Nerur in Tiruchi district. It belongs to 11th century A.D. Kṛṣṇa is depicted showing *abhaya-hasta* with his right arm. His left leg is lifted up in an unusual pose, while the right foot is placed down. His headgear, a sort of *karaṇḍa-makuṭa*, is rather peculiar and certainly very beautiful (Fig. 38). Two more specimens of the bronze image of dancing Kṛṣṇa are illustrated here. Both of them belong to the Chōḷa period but display two different poses—one has left foot lifted up and other the right foot (Figs. 39 and 40).

The Nardhana Kṛṣṇa from unknown locality is a typical Chōḷa bronze image. Kṛṣṇa is shown wearing another type of crown, along with other jewels. His right arm shows *abhaya-mudrā* and his right leg is lifted up (Fig. 41). The dancing Kṛṣṇa is also available on stone sculptures (Fig. 42) at Srinivasanallur, Tiruchi district.

(10) Kāliyamardana Kṛṣṇa

As already pointed out, the earliest sculptural representations of this theme are found in the Pallava period and from early Chōḷa period, we begin to get exquisite bronze representations of this theme. This is again a unique contribution of Tamil artists for we hardly have bronze figure of Kāliyamardana anywhere else.

A stone relief sculpture of Kāliyamardana in the temple of Sriperumbudur is illustrated here. Kṛṣṇa is holding the tail of the snake with his left hand and his right arm is touching its head (Fig. 43).

An exquisite bronze sculpture of Kāliya Kṛṣṇa belonging to early Chōḷa period (10th century) is also illustrated here. Kṛṣṇa, as a youth, is very beautiful to look at. Here, Kāliya is personified and is shown in *anjali* form. Kṛṣṇa wears the *channavira*, beautiful *hāras* and *kaṭi-sūtra* and has his right arm in *abhaya*. It shows supple modelling and restrained ornamentation and remarkable balance (Fig. 44).

Another bronze figure (Fig. 45) illustrated here is also a good example of the Chōḷa style. Its locality is however not known. The *patrakuṇḍalas* are prominently shown.

A 13th century (Pāṇḍya) bronze image of Kṛṣṇa dancing on the snake Kāliya is found in the temple of Tiruppullani near Ramesvaram. Kṛṣṇa's left leg is placed on the snake's hoods, his left arm is holding its tail while his right leg is slightly raised and his right arm is in the *abhaya-mudrā* (Fig. 46).

Two good examples of the same theme in Vijayanagar style are illustrated here from Sundaraperumāḷ temple, Thanjavur district. Kṛṣṇa is richly decorated and is shown dancing on the snake. The Kāliya is lying down with his hands raised above in *anjali-mudrā* (Fig. 47). The next piece illustrated here is a good example of the Vijayanagar style with more ornamental details (Fig. 48).

A popular way of depicting Kṛṣṇa as Kāliyamardana is to show him dancing on the coiled snakes. This is usually kept on the banks of a tank along with the *nāga* stones for worship. It is commonly met with in all the villages (Fig. 49). Two beautiful Pāṇḍyan metal images of the same theme i.e. Kṛṣṇa dancing with the snakes have come from Ādi-Jagannātha Temple,

Tiruppullani. It is a rare representation of Kṛṣṇa associated with the *nāgas* in the bronze medium (Figs. 50 and 51).

(11) Vēṇugōpāla (Kuḻal-ūthum-piḷḷai)

Another popular theme of Kṛṣṇa's boyhood is Kṛṣṇa as a flute player Vēṇugōpāla or Gānagōpāla. The *Kuḻalūthum-piḷḷai* form was a favourite one with the Āḻvārs. The Tamil term frequently occurs in inscriptions also. Stone or metal images of Kṛṣṇa playing on a flute are found in plenty. Sometimes he is shown with two or more hands surrounded by cattle. Chaturbhuja Vēṇugōpāla and Aṣṭabhuja Vēṇugōpāla representations became very popular during the Vijayanagar times.

The Vēṇugōpāla sculpture in stone from Sārangapāni Temple of Kumbakonam is one of the best examples of Chōḷa period. It is a two-armed image of Kṛṣṇa with crossed legs and surrounded by shepherds and cattle (Fig. 52). Another stone sculpture of Chaturbhuja Vēṇugōpāla of later Chōḷa period is kept in the National Museum, New Delhi (Fig. 53).

An exquisite two-armed metal image of Kṛṣṇa with slightly bent legs is shown here. It belongs to the late Chōḷa period and is found at Nāgapattinam (Fig. 54).

The beautiful metal image of Kṛṣṇa found at Adi Jagannathaswami Temple, Tiruppullani has four arms: two arms hold the *sankha* and *chakra*, while another pair of arms are shown as playing on the flute. His right leg is bent backwards and touches the left leg. This Pāṇḍyan bronze is a rich feast to the eyes (Fig. 55) with an impressive expression characteristic of Kṛṣṇa idol in this pose, luring the whole cowherd community and the animals alike and at the same time showing the divinity of the deity. The image is accommodated in a beautiful *prabhāvaḷi* emanating from the mouth of *makaras*.

The Vēṇugōpāla shrine at Srirangam has many different postures of Vēṇugōpāla in its niches. This shrine has been ascribed to the Hoysala period (13th century). One example of the exquisite Chaturbhuja-Vēṇugōpāla is illustrated here (Fig. 56).

The beautiful stone sculpture of four-armed Vēṇugōpāla found in Trivikrama temple at Tirukkōvalūr is illustrated here (Fig. 57). Tirukkōvalūr is one of the Pancha-Kṛṣṇa-kshētras.

A sculpture on a pillar in the temple of Tiruvidandai shows Kṛṣṇa as playing on the flute with a cow licking his leg (Fig. 58). Two other exquisite relief sculptures of Chaturbhuja Vēṇugōpāla in the Vijayanagar style are found at Jalakantēsvara temple, Vellore and Paḍaivēḍu respectively (Figs. 59 and 60).

A bronze image of Chaturbhuja Vēṇugōpāla belonging to the 17th century is found in the Chennai Museum (Fig. 61). Another beautiful bronze of the Chōḷa period is found at Tiruvendipuram (Fig. 62).

A late Pāṇḍyan or Nāyak specimen of sculpture representing Aṣṭabhuja Vēṇugōpāla surrounded by his female admirers (gōpis) is found at Srīvaikuntam near Tirunelveli. A similar group is found at Tirukkodikāval, Thanjavur district (Fig. 63). A large-sized but beautiful sculpture of Vēṇugōpāla in the Nāyak style is found at Āṇḍāḷ temple, Srivilliputtur (Fig. 64).

(12) Kṛṣṇa as Madanagōpāla (Fig. 65)

Another rare form of Kṛṣṇa is that of Madanagōpāla a combination of Kṛṣṇa and Madana or Manmatha. A magnificent example of this form is found at Viswanātha temple, Tenkasi belonging to the Nāyak period (17th century). He is eight-armed, one of them having a prominent sugarcane bow and arrow, typical for Manmatha.

An interesting sculpture on a pillar of Sri Varadarājaswāmi temple, Kānchipuram shows Kṛṣṇa as Aṣṭabhuja Vēṇugōpāla i.e. with eight arms having a number of weapons like bow and arrow, sword, shield, *sankha* and *chakra.* It can also be identified as Madanagōpāla and it belongs to the middle of 16th century (Fig. 66).

(13) Kṛṣṇa in the Vastrāpaharaṇa Scene

Once, the shepherd maidens were taking bath in the Yamuna leaving their clothes on the banks of the river. Kṛṣṇa, in order to tease them, took all their clothes and climbed to the top of the tree. When the girls begged of Kṛṣṇa to return their clothes as they were naked, Kṛṣṇa refused to give their clothes unless they came out of the water, raise their hands and do *anjali* to him. This they did to satisfy him and got back their clothes. This episode is the subject of many interesting sculptures. Four such specimens are illustrated here—two from Varadarājaswāmi Temple, Kānchi (Figs. 67 and 68), one from Vellore (Fig. 69) and one from Tiruvadandai (Fig. 70). All of them are of the Vijayanagar period (16th century). Though the theme is same, the mode of depiction varies from one another.

(14) Kṛṣṇa as the Cowherd King (Rājagōpāla or Rājamannār)

Kṛṣṇa as Rājamannār is a rare form in bronze found only in Tamilnāḍu. This form of Kṛṣṇa with or without his consorts became a favourite one with the artists during the time of the Chōḷas. The famous Rājagōpālaswāmi temple of Mannārgudi, the Kāṭṭumannār Temple of Kāṭṭumannārgudi and the Rājagōpālaswāmi temple of Maṇimangalam are the best examples of that style. Kṛṣṇa, the king among the cowherds, is depicted with two arms, left arm bent as if leaning on a cow and the right arm shown in *kaṭaka-hasta* to hold a stick or a hook to graze the cattle.

Six representative examples of bronze figures and one of stone are illustrated here. All of them (except one, which is from Pāṇḍyan country) are fine products of the Chōḷa period. The sculpture from Chidambaram, now kept in the Government Museum, Chennai, is a rare and beautiful specimen (Fig. 71). Kṛṣṇa stands in a *tribhanga* pose with the shepherd's hook in his right hand and embracing Satyabhāmā or Nappinnai with the other. He wears the *patrakuṇḍalas* and peacock feather type of coiffure on his head. This is datable to the 13th century.

Among the bronze images illustrated here, the most famous one is the beautiful *utsava* image of Rājamannār at Mannārgudi (Fig. 72) of the Chōḷa period. The next one from the Sundaraperumāḷ temple (Thanjavur) has been dated by Douglas Barrett to A.D. 1040.[7] It shows the *kēsabandha* type of coiffure and restrained ornamentation and very supple modelling (Fig. 73). Close to this in point of time and style, is the exquisite Rājamannār group from Ādikudi (Tiruchi district). Here Rājagōpāla stands gracefully flanked by his consorts Rukmini and Satyabhāmā on either side (Fig. 74). His left arm rests on the cow and his right arm holds a long and artistically designed hook. He has the *kēsabandha* with peacock feather, *patrakuṇḍala*, *hāras*, beautiful *kaṭisūtra* and the *yajnopavīta*. The whole group has been very proportionately designed and tastefully executed, characteristic of the Chōḷa bronzes of the 11th century.[8]

The next group illustrated here is from Seramadevi, Tirunelveli district (Fig. 75). But the Pāṇḍyan artists have also more or less followed the Chōḷa pattern and this group closely resembles the Ādikudi example cited above. All the three figures have the *kēsabandha* type of coiffure. Both the consorts are shown without the *kuchabandha* (breast band) unlike some Chōḷa examples where distinction is shown between Rukmini and Satyabhāmā. Nevertheless, this group has been carefully modelled and gracefully executed.

An impressive group of Chōḷa bronzes of Rājamannār in the company of his consorts and Garuḍa is now found in the Los Angeles County Museum of Art, U.S.A. (Fig. 76). Pratapaditya Pal, who has written a monograph on this group, has convincingly dated it to A.D. 1100.[9] It has been made exactly as prescribed in the *Vaikānasa-āgama*. Here, Rājagōpāla stands gracefully with his left hand resting on the shoulders of Satyabhāmā and right hand in the *kaṭaka-hasta* to hold the hook. The presence of Garuḍa is specifically mentioned in the *āgama*. Here, Rukmini is shown with the *kuchabandha* whereas

Satyabhāmā is without it. The latter is equated with Bhū-dēvi and the former with Srī-dēvi. Unfortunately, the findspot of the bronzes is lost to us but there is no doubt that they are from Tamilnāḍu and belong to the middle Chōḷa period. Two more bronzes of Rājagōpāla are also illustrated here, one from Nilappadi, Tiruchi district and datable to 12th century and the other now kept in the National Museum, New Delhi (Figs. 77 and 78).

(15) Gopi-Kṛṣṇa Love Scenes

Kṛṣṇa as a divine lover is yet another favourite subject of the poets as well as the artists. His amorous acts, his enchanting sports with the *gōpikās*, his *rāsa*-dance with the cowherd girls are all sung by the Āḷvārs and others. Here some of the love scenes of Kṛṣṇa depicted in sculptures are illustrated. The sculpture of Kṛṣṇa playing on the flute, with two *gōpikās* on each side dancing, from Srivaikuntam temple has already been cited.

Another illustration given here shows the Hōli festival during which colour-water is sprayed on each other, through a syringe. The Hōli sport was played by Kṛṣṇa with Rādhā and other *gōpikās*. The sculpture in the Sēshasāyī-*maṇḍapa* in the Ranganātha temple, Srirangam gives a beautiful picture of this sport (Fig. 79). A unique sculpture in Ādinātha temple, Āḷvār Thirunagiri, shows Kṛṣṇa and his consorts dancing. Kṛṣṇa is holding their hands and all the three are standing on one leg. The sculpture forms a window panel in the temple (see Fig. 3 above).

The relief sculpture on a pillar in the Varadarajaswami Temple, Kanchipuram shows Kṛṣṇa making love to Rādhā (Fig. 80). Kṛṣṇa hugging his sweetheart (identified as Rukmini by the local belief) is found in the Ramaswamy temple, Kumbakonam (Fig. 81).

(16) Kṛṣṇa as the Teacher of the Bhagavat-Gītā (Gītāchārya)

The divine personality of Kṛṣṇa is fully revealed in his role as Gītāchārya. Kṛṣṇa as the expounder or teacher of the *Bhagavat Gītā* is worshipped in a few places in Tamilnāḍu. Many sculptural representations are also available. For instance, a seated Kṛṣṇa figure in stone from Perambalur depicts him teaching the *Gītā*. His right arm is showing *vyākhyāna-mudrā*, and his left arm *varadamudrā* (Fig. 82).

Another interesting sculpture, illustrated here, is a bronze from Ennayiram, South Arcot district. The seated Kṛṣṇa is shown with four arms, two holding the *sankha* and *chakra*, one of the other two showing *sūchihasta* and the fourth one hanging on the left knee. This beautiful bronze image shows Kṛṣṇa in his divine form (Fig. 83).

(17) Kṛṣṇa as Pārthasārathi

This is the representation of Kṛṣṇa as a charioteer of Pārtha or Arjuna. The main deity of Pārthasārathi Temple, Triplicane, Chennai is an outstanding example. Here, the *mūlavar* stands majestically with two arms: the right hand bears the conch (*sankha*) which is unusual and the other is in the *abhaya-mudrā* (Fig. 84). The *utsavabhēra* is an excellent image of the middle Chōḷa period (about 1100 A.D.). It is four-armed with *sankha, chakra, abhaya* and the *gadā*. His face has a number of potholes believed to represent the scars left by the arrows which were shot at him on the Kurukshetra battlefield. This is a very unique representation of Pārthasārathi not found elsewhere (Fig. 85).

(18) Ananta Kṛṣṇa

A rare piece of bronze sculpture has come down to us from the Nagaraja temple, Nagarkoil (Kanyakumari district) depicting Kṛṣṇa and his two consorts with Nāga hoods on their heads. He is locally called Anantakṛṣṇa, Ananta being another name of his serpent Ādisēsha. Ananta Kṛṣṇa is shown with two arms, his right arm in *abhaya-mudrā* and his left arm showing *kaṭi-hasta* (Fig. 86). A similar form of Kṛṣṇa with Rukmini and Satyabhāmā is worshipped in the Rājagōpāla Temple, Mannārgudi in Thanjavur district.

(19) Kṛṣṇa as Viṭṭōbha or Paṇḍarinātha

As already mentioned, Kṛṣṇa as Pāṇḍuranga Viṭṭala, the presiding deity at Pandaripura in Maharashtra, was introduced in South India during the Vijayanagar and Mahratta rule. The Viṭṭala Temple at Humpi is famous. There is a shrine for Viṭṭala Kṛṣṇa at Srirangam. There are also villages in Tamilnāḍu named as Viṭṭalapuram (in Tirunelveli and Chengalpattu districts). The sculpture illustrated here is from a Viṣṇu temple at Kānchi ascribable to the 16th century. Viṭṭala is standing with left hand holding a conch and right arm in *varada* (Fig. 87).

Kṛṣṇa Theme in Paintings

A noteworthy development in the field of art during the Vijayanagar and Nāyak times is the appearance of wall paintings of Kṛṣṇa's life and deeds in various temples of South India. This corresponds to the vast array of the Mughal and Rajasthani miniature paintings of Kṛṣṇa theme that appeared in North India in the 16th and 17th centuries.

In the Varadarājaswāmi Temple, Kānchi, we see a fine panel of paintings on the ceiling depicting Kṛṣṇa's youthful sports like Vastrāpaharaṇa, Kāliya-mardana and Vēṇugōpāla. They are in Vijayanagar style and ascribable to the 16th century A.D. (Fig. 88). Beautiful paintings of Kṛṣṇa's *bāla-līlās*, showing Chakatāsura-vadha, Kēsi-vadha, and Dhenuka-vadha can be seen in the Jain temple at Tirupparuttikunram near Kānchi. The paintings belong to Nāyak period (Fig. 89). This shows the association of Kṛṣṇa with the Jain mythology and he was held in high esteem by the Jainas.[10]

Two more paintings illustrated here are from the Ranganāthaswāmi temple, Srirangam. The first one (Fig. 90) shows Kṛṣṇa seated and surrounded by his consorts. The other one depicts Kṛṣṇa with his consorts (Fig. 91). Both the paintings show fine composition, exquisite dresses and ornaments and are ascribable to the late Hoysala or early Vijayanagar period (14th century A.D.).[11]

The most popular paintings of Kṛṣṇa are from Thanjavur school of Mahraṭṭas, showing Kṛṣṇa with a butter pot—Veṇṇaithāḷi Kaṇṇan (Fig. 92). We can see this picture almost in every home in Tamilnāḍu. During the annual festival of Viṣṇu temples, the presiding deity is dressed up as *Veṇṇai-thāḷi* Kṛṣṇa and is taken in procession. Devotees offer butter to the deity (for instance, Pārthasārathi temple, Triplicane). An interesting point is that even in Subrahmanya Temple at Tiruchendur, Kumāra Vitankar is dressed up as Kṛṣṇa with butter pot on the 5th day of the annual Māṣi festival. This shows Kṛṣṇa as a divine child is very popular all over Tamilnāḍu and worshipped by the Vaiṣṇavas and Saivas without difference. Recently some late but good paintings (18th century) of Bhagavata scenes were discovered in the Varadarāja temple, Kānchipuram (Figs. 101 and 102).

Ivory and Wood Carvings

There is a unique set of ivory images of Kṛṣṇa in intimate company of Rādhā and Rukmini preserved in Sri Ranganātha temple, Srirangam. They were presented to the temple by Thanjavur Nāyak kings in the 17th century. Interestingly Kṛṣṇa is shown in the typical costumes of the Nāyak times (Figs. 93 and 94).

Wood carvings of Kṛṣṇa story are commonly met with in the wooden cars of the Vaiṣṇava temples all over South India. Good examples of such wood carvings can be seen in the cars of Sri Varadarājaswāmi Temple, Kānchi, Sārangapāni Temple, Kumbakonam, Ranganāthaswāmi Temple, Srirangam, Āṇḍāḷ Temple, Srivilliputtur, Rājagōpālaswāmi Temple, Mannārkudi. They are usually found in relief panels in the basement (*adhiṣṭhāna*) portion of the temple cars. Here four specimens from the wooden chariot at Rājagōpālaswāmi temple, Mannārkudi are illustrated, each one depicting a memorable scene from Kṛṣṇa's life. They are: Kṛṣṇa holding the butter pot (Fig. 95), Kṛṣṇa killing the demon Pūthaki by sucking her blood (Fig. 96), Kṛṣṇa killing the elephant Kuvalayāpiṭa (Fig. 97), Kṛṣṇa as a charioteer of Arjuna (Fig. 98). We see similar beautiful wood carvings of Kṛṣṇa's life in the wooden chariot of Varadarājaswāmi Temple at Kānchi (Fig. 99).

The last but not the least specimen of Yasōdā Kṛṣṇa illustrated here is found popular at folk level and similar ones are made even today (Fig. 100).

References

1. Raman, K.V., *Sri Varadarājaswāmi Temple, Kānchi*, Chapter V.
2. Ramachandran, T.N., *Tirupparuttikunram and its Temples* (Madras Museum Publication).
3. Chitra Viji, *Srirangam Paintings* (Ph.D. thesis of Madras University, unpublished).
4. Srinivasan, K.R., *Cave Temples of the Pallavas.*
5. Sivaramamurti, C., *Mamallapuram*, New Delhi, 1978.
6. Srinivasan, K.R., *Dharmarāja-Ratha.*

6a. Dennis Hudson, *The Srimad Bhagavata Purana in Stone* (*J. of Vaisnava Studies*, Vol. 3, No. 3); *Vasudeva Kṛṣṇa in Theology and Architecture, op. cit.*, Vol. 2, No. 1, 1993.

7. Barrett, Douglas, *Early Chōḷa Bronzes.*
8. Two more bronzes of Rājamannār of the middle Chōḷa period are described by P.R. Srinivasan, *Bronzes of South India*, Figs. 328, 329 and 330.
9. Pratapaditya Pal, *Kṛṣṇa: The Cowherd King*, Los Angeles County Museum of Art Monograph Series, No. 1.
10. Ramachandran, T.N., *op. cit.*
11. Chitra Viji, *op. cit.*

EPILOGUE

The historical data from different sources—literature, epigraphy, temple-myths and traditions and the numerous religious and art specimens presented in the foregoing pages would amply attest to the deep-rooted character of Kṛṣṇa worship in Tamilnāḍu. In the first chapter, we have clearly shown how the ancient Tamil works of the Sangam period contain voluminous references to the popularity of Kṛṣṇa who was known by his many endearing names (Māyōn, Māyavan, Māl) and whose boyhood sports were very familiar to the Tamil society. The pastoral origin of Kṛṣṇa appealed to the Tamil people who honoured him as the presiding deity of the *mullai* (forest) region as attested by the *Tolkāppiyam.* Māyōn is the Tamil equivalent of Kṛṣṇa (black) in Sanskrit and it was applied to Viṣṇu. We have cited evidence to show how the Sangam literature identified Kṛṣṇa as an *avatāra* of Viṣṇu. Kṛṣṇa worship probably reached the Tamil country after the identification of Vēdic God Viṣṇu with the Vṛṣṇi hero Vāsudēva-Kṛṣṇa had taken place in North India.

The *Puranānūru* mentions Kṛṣṇa, Balarāma, Siva and Muruga as the leading gods.[1] Another verse in the same collection refers to Balarāma and Kṛṣṇa as the "two great gods" (*iru-perum-daivam*) and compares the Chōḷa and the Pāṇḍyan kings to them.[2] We have also pointed out how the Balarāma-Kṛṣṇa combination frequently occurs in the Sangam works[3] and it is a pointer to the impact of the *Panchavīra* or Vṛṣṇi hero-cult that was popular in the Mathura region around the second and first centuries B.C. The *Paripāḍal* makes a pointed reference to the members of Vṛṣṇi clan—the dark complexioned Vāsudēva (Kṛṣṇa), the white complexioned Baladēva, the green complexioned Pradyumna (Kṛṣṇa's son) and Aniruddha (Kṛṣṇa's grandson). They formed the nucleus of the *Pancha-vīra*[4] or Pāncharātra worship, an important feature of the Bhāgavata school. So, the *Paripāḍal* clearly attests to the impact of Bhāgavatism in the Tamil country. We have also shown how in the earlier Sangam works like the *Ahanānūru* and the *Kalithokai* several episodes connected with Kṛṣṇa's life are frequently alluded to. Some customs peculiar to the *mullai* region of Tamilnāḍu like the fight with the seven bulls before marriage are given and the bull fight arena is likened to the battle-ground of Kurukshētra. *Kalithokai* mentions a number of episodes from the *Mahābhārata* while the *Puranānūru* seems to mention the *Gītā* in one of the verses.[5]

In the first chapter it is shown in a separate section how eloquent is the Tamil epic *Silappadikāram* (5th or 6th century A.D.) on the many-faceted greatness of Kṛṣṇa. It extolls him as the mighty one who once churned the milky ocean but who submissively allowed his hands to be tied (by his mother Yasōdā in his Kṛṣṇāvatāra). "What is the use of those eyes which have not seen Kariavan (Kṛṣṇa), the ears which have not heard of His greatness, the tongue which has not sung the praise of the feet of the Lord who went as a humble messenger for the Pāṇḍavas?"[6] The details of Kṛṣṇa's life as given in the epic have already been discussed in the section, and need not be repeated here. The *Āichiyar Kuravai* chapter describes the enchanting dance which Kṛṣṇa, Nappinnai and Balarāma performed at Āyarpāḍi (Gōkulam). The association of Nappinnai, the beloved shepherd girl with Kṛṣṇa is peculiar to Tamil tradition like the association of the huntress Vaḷḷi with Muruga. According to some scholars, the Rādhā cult of later times was close to the ancient Nappinnai cult of Tamilnāḍu.

The epic also mentions the several peculiar dance forms—*alliyam, mallāḍal, kudakūttu*, performed by Kṛṣṇa. But all of them are associated with his heroic deeds. This differs from the *rāsa-krīḍā* dance with which Kṛṣṇa is associated in the north. In the latter, it is related to Kṛṣṇa's youthful and romantic plays with the cowherd girls whereas the Tamil literature describes the dances with heroic (*puram*) deeds. This is one of the many instances to show that Kṛṣṇa life-stories were adapted to suit the Tamil tradition.

We have also discussed the close association of the Tamil kings like the Pāṇḍyas and the Āy Vēḷirs with the Kṛṣṇa worship. The former claim descent from Neḍiyōn "with the beautiful garland on his neck", a description which is also given for Māyōn in other contexts indicating that Neḍiyōn and Māyōn were one and the same, Viṣṇu or Kṛṣṇa. The references to the Pāṇḍyas as the Panchavar, the five Pāṇḍava brothers of the *Mahābhārata* fame and the devotion of a Pāṇḍya king (Iḷam Peruvaḷudi) to the temples of Balarāma and Kṛṣṇa at Māl-irum-kunru (Alagarkōil near Madurai) mentioned in the *Paripāḍal* are also significant. The claim of the Pāṇḍya kings in their copper plate grants of 8th century that they established the Sangam (Tamil academy) at Madurai and translated the *Mahābhārata* into Tamil is also significant. In fact, there is some basis for the theory that Madurai, the capital of the Pāṇḍyas, was possibly named after Mathura, the birth place of Kṛṣṇa. Hence, the Tamil works and inscriptions refer to Madurai as the "Southern Madurai" (*Ten-Madurai*), and the one in the north as "Northern Madurai" (*Vada Madurai*).[7] In fact, a verse in the *Kalithokai* mentions the Pāṇḍyas as belonging to the cowherd clan,[8] and the *Silappadikāram* describes the Pāṇḍyan king as none other than Kṛṣṇa.[9]

The association of the Āy Vēḷirs with the Yādava clan and Kṛṣṇa worship is another important feature that comes out boldly in the Sangam literature. We have cited the evidence from the poem of Kapilar which alludes to migration of the Āy Vēḷirs from the Dwārakā region to South India. The Āy Vēḷir chieftains, who settled down in Āy country (near Kanyakumari), were quite prominent in Tamilnāḍu during the Sangam age. We have already pointed out their long and historic association with Kṛṣṇa cult during the Sangam and later times too.[10] It is quite possible that they played an important part in introducing and popularising the Kṛṣṇa worship as the Lord of the *mullai* region which they occupied. Thus, we see that the ancient Sangam literature is a rich source of valuable information on the advent of the Kṛṣṇa worship in Tamilnāḍu and the process of its adaptation and assimilation into the Tamil cultural and religious milieu.

The next stage in the development of Kṛṣṇa worship is associated with the Bhakti movement in Tamilnāḍu from about 7th to 9th century A.D., championed by the Tamil Vaiṣṇava saints called the Āḷvārs. They carried on the eclectic tenets of the Bhāgavata tradition and preached a simple religion, based on love and devotion (*Bhakti*) free from ritual barriers and caste differences. Many of them belonged to the lower castes. The personality of Kṛṣṇa in his simple and enchanting forms served as their focal centre. Their hymns (*Divyaprabandham*) glorify Kṛṣṇa as the Supreme Lord who came down to the earth as the saviour of mankind and the refuge of the good, the lowly and the devoted. His qualities of humility in serving his true devotees like Arjuna (as his charioteer) and the Pāṇḍavas (as their messenger) are extolled as well as his divine and transcendental qualities (*paratva*). Periyāḷvār assumed the role of Yasōdā and showed his motherly feelings for child Kṛṣṇa (*mātru-vātsalya*) through his inimitable Tamil poems in *pillai-Tamil.* Other Āḷvārs like Nammāḷvār, Āṇḍāḷ and Tirumangai have enjoyed his beauty in the ancient Tamil *Aham* poetic tradition (in the *talaivan-talaivi* or *nāyaka-nāyaki bhāva*) of taking the role of a lovelorn lady longing for the union with her beloved. Āṇḍāḷ or Godha has described her dream-marriage with beloved Kṛṣṇa in a beautiful poem (*Vāranamāyiram*) which is popularly sung in the Vaiṣṇava marriages in South India even now as a sacred ritual. The Tamils have honoured Āṇḍāḷ or Kōthai-Nāchiār as the incarnation of Bhū-dēvi and deified her in a shrine placed on the left side of Viṣṇu's shrine.

The emotional sentiments couched in simple and beautiful Tamil hymns of the Āḷvārs contributed greatly to the popularisation of Vaiṣṇavism and the *Purāṇic* stories with Kṛṣṇa as a central figure. It influenced many contemporary Pāṇḍyan and Pallava rulers who called themselves as Parama-Bhāgavatas and extended their patronage to the movement by raising temples for Viṣṇu and Kṛṣṇa at places like Kānchi, Māmallapuram, Tiruvallikkēni and Tiruvellarai. The temple and the icon therein began to assume greater importance as a result of the Āḷvārs' appeal to the people to go to the temples to worship the Lord enshrined there. The temples sung by them came to be glorified as the *Divya-dēsas* (holy shrines). Their hymns also contributed to the localisation of Kṛṣṇa's life episodes in Tamilnāḍu. Their movement marked a turning point in the religious history of Tamilnāḍu in stemming the tide of heterodox religions (like Buddhism and Jainism) and propagating the ideals of Bhāgavatism. In fact, the *Bhāgavata-Purāṇa,* according to many scholars, was written in South India and contains clear influences of the Tamil hymns of the Āḷvārs.

During the post-Bhakti period we see the full impact of the Āḷvārs' movement on the Vaiṣṇava leaders like Yāmunā, Rāmānuja and Vēdānta Dēsika. In their works Kṛṣṇa as the Lord who taught the *Gītā* (*Gītāchārya*) looms large. Yāmuna wrote his *Gītāsangraha,* Rāmānuja his *Gītā-Bhāshya,* Vēdānta Dēsika the *Gītā-tātparyachandrika.* If the Āḷvārs' approach can be described as emotional *Bhakti,* the approach of the *Āchāryas* can be described as intellectual *Bhakti.* Their works reflect an important stage in the development of Sri-Vaiṣṇava theology of the Rāmānuja school which had profound influence on many Bhakti schools of later times. They emphasised the Bhakti Yōga and the *prapatti-mārga* (path of surrender) as central to the *Gītā* and the *Bhāgavata Purāṇa.* We have already shown how the *āchāyas* have expressed their deep devotion to Kṛṣṇa through their brilliant commentaries (*vyākhyānas*) and discourses.

At the same time, the reverence and esteem with which Kṛṣṇa was held in the Tamil society can be gleaned from the numerous Tamil works like Perundevanar's *Bhāratam* (9th century) and Villiputtūrār's *Bhāratam* (15th century) which have a high place in Tamil literary and religious history. The *Bhagavat Gītā* was also translated into Tamil by Sri Baṭṭanār and the *Bhāgavatam* by Chevvai Sūduvār (17th century). We have shown how Kṛṣṇa's personality and teachings have inspired generations of Tamil poets, philosophers and religious leaders over the centuries. Even in the present century Subrahmania Bhārati, hailed as the father of Tamil literary renaissance, has left immortal poems on Kṛṣṇa. The *Mahābhārata* story has percolated to the folk level through the street dramas (*therukūthu*) so popular in the villages of Tamilnāḍu. There are numerous temples for the *Mahābhārata* characters like Dharmarāja and Draupadi Amman in the villages of Tamilnāḍu.

During the Bhakti and the post-Bhakti periods (from 600 A.D. onwards) several beautiful temples for Kṛṣṇa were built in many parts of Tamilnāḍu (as detailed in Chapter IV). The innumerable inscriptions and the *Sthalapurāṇas* throw light on their history and traditions. From them we learn of the extensive patronage extended to them not only by the kings and the elite but also by the common folk like the shepherd class, the agriculturists, the artisans and the merchants. Several festivals (like *Kṛṣṇa-Jayanti*) and rituals in honour of Kṛṣṇa were celebrated. The inscriptions also reveal that Kṛṣṇa was identified and deified with his several endearing Tamil names like *Tirukuḷal-ūdum-*

piḷḷai (the divine flute player), *Veṇṇai-kūthan* (the butter-dancer), *Kuḍakkūthan* (the pot-dancer), *Kariamāṇikkam* (the black gem), *Alcgia-mannār* (the beautiful shepherd).

The interesting process of localisation is also seen in naming places after the holy places connected with Kṛṣṇa. Mannārgudi (Thanjavur Dt.) where there is a famous temple for Rājagōpāla is described as the Southern Dwārakā, Tiruvallekēni (Triplicane) as the Brindāraṇya-kshētra, Tirukkōvalūr as Kṛṣṇāraṇya-kshētra and several other places as Tiruvāypāḍi (Gōkulam). The inscriptions and the temple myths clearly indicate how Kṛṣṇa worship became well integrated with the temple-centred religion and culture of the Tamils in the medieval times.

The copious religious and literary productions on Kṛṣṇa are equally matched by the impressive array of sculptures and icons that came up in an uninterrupted flow in Tamilnāḍu. In the last chapter we have demonstrated how the Kṛṣṇa theme inspired the Tamil artists—stone and metal icon-makers, painters, wood and ivory carvers through many centuries. We have many superb masterpieces of the Pallava period like the large sculptural panel of Kṛṣṇa as Gōvardhanadhāri at Māmallapuram (the like of which is not to be seen anywhere in India in size or beauty), Kāliya-Kṛṣṇa in the Dharmarāja-ratha at Māmallapuram and Vaikuṇṭaperumāḷ Temple, Kānchi. In the Chōḷa period, we see the stone and metal sculptors vying with one another in giving expression to complex and difficult themes. Bold experimentation was made in metal casting and as a result, we have several masterpieces of bronze icons depicting Kṛṣṇa as Santānagōpāla, Bālakṛṣṇa, Navanīta-Nāṭya Kṛṣṇa, Rājagōpāla, Vēnugōpāla, Pārthasārathi, Gītāchārya, hardly to be seen anywhere in India quantitatively or qualitatively. They display the artists' creative and innovative genius and skill for powerful modelling and graceful execution. We have already illustrated and discussed as many as hundred selected specimens to show the continuous flow of the Kṛṣṇa theme in Tamil art and the changing styles and the new forms that were incorporated from time to time. To cite an example, the icon of Rājamannār or Rājagōpāla (Kṛṣṇa as a king of cowherds) and Santāna-Kṛṣṇa became very popular during the Chōḷa period. There were more temples for Vēnugōpāla during the Vijayanagar times. The cult of Kṛṣṇa as Vittōba was introduced in Tamilnāḍu during the Vijayanagar times.

There are rare and excellent paintings of the *Bhāgavata Purāṇa* and *Kṛṣṇa-līlās* in the temples of Tamilnāḍu datable to a period from the 14th to 17th century at places like Srīrangam, Kānchi, Alagarkōil, Ādamankottai (Dharmapuri Dt.). Many of them were done under the patronage of the Vijayanagar and Nāyak kings (Figs. 101 and 102). The rich wood carvings seen in the temple cars of the Vaiṣṇava centres at Srīrangam, Kānchi,

Mannārgudi, Srīvilliputtūr also attest to the profound influence of the Kṛṣṇa theme in the art productions of the Tamil country.

Thus, we can see how the Kṛṣṇa cult had a long history in Tamilnāḍu with its roots going deep into the Sangam age and how through the centuries it had grown and permeated into the religious, literary, artistic and cultural heritage of the Tamils. Kṛṣṇa worship continues to be a vibrant and popular one cutting across sectarian differences and the discourses on his life and teachings through the *Bhāgavatam*, the *Mahābhāratam*, the *Bhagavat Gītā* and the Āḻvārs' hymns continue to attract the devotion of the Tamils.

References

1. *PRN*, 56.
2. *Ibid.*, 58.
3. *PRP*, 3; 11: 81-82.
4. The four together with Kṛṣṇa's grandson Sātyaki formed the Pancha-vīras which constitute the Pancha-vyūha forms of Viṣṇu.
5. See Chapter I.
6. *SLP*, *Āichiyar Kuravāi* section, V.35, 36 and 37.
7. *Tiruppāvai*, V.5.
8. *Kali.*, 105:1-7.
9. *SLP*, XVII-V.29.
10. Vide Chapter I.

APPENDIX

TAMIL POEMS ON KṚṢṆA— SELECT EXCERPTS

Silappadikāram on Kṛṣṇa/Viṣṇu

(From Canto 17, *Ācchiyarkuravai,* the Dance of the Cowgirls)

Friends! Māyavan (Kṛṣṇa) swung a calf like a slung stone and knocked down all the orchard's fruit. If he came down to see our herd, then we could hear the lovely sound of his most wondrous flute.

xxxx xxxx

How can we describe the face of the lovely girl (Pinnai) distressed by the remorse of him who stole her dress?

How can we describe the loveliness of her who stole the heart of him?

xxxx xxxx

God! A lotus springs forth from your navel. Your hands that once churned the ocean were tied by Yasoda with a churning rope. Is that an example of your magic? Your designs are ever mysterious.

xxxx xxxx

Vain are the ears that are not filled with great doings of the hero who, in three strides, encompassed the three worlds.

Vain are the eyes that do not see the god, the dark god, the mysterious god.

Vain is the tongue that does not sing the praise of Him who countered Kamsa's dark intrigues. Accompanied by singing of the Vedas he went to meet the hundred Kauravas as messenger from the five brothers.

Vain is the tongue that does not sing the praise of Him Narayana, the shelter of mankind. May the God we honour through his love-dance here show mercy on us now, for fear has spread upon our herds (Translation by Alain Danielou in his book *Shilappadikāram* (*The Ankle Bracelet,* pp. 115-120, A New Directions Book, New York, 1965).

Periyāḷvār

Viṣṇuchitta renowned as Periyāḷvār has poured out his heart on his favourite deity Kṛṣṇa in hundreds of beautiful verses in his *Tirumoḻi.* Those which he sang assuming the role of mother Yasoda are unique and best examples of the Tamil literary genre called *Piḷḷai-Tamiḻ* where the mother goes into raptures enjoying her child's bewitching beauty at different stages of its growth from the cradle to adulthood. It includes the cradle songs (lullaby), and songs for giving oil-bath, dressing, feeding, calling the moon to play etc. A free translation of some of his verses exemplifying the mother's love (*mātru-vātsalya*) is given below:

Yasoda calls all her friends, the cowherd women in great excitement to come and enjoy the many-faceted charms of the personality of the child from the foot to head (*pādāti-kēsam*). She says: "You all come and see how he enjoys putting his toe into his mouth; the charm of his ankles with tinkling silver anklets (and asleep after drinking my breast-milk sumptuously); the fine navel of the child who showed his valour during his plays with his friends like a baby tusker; the splendid shoulders of the one who within four or five months of his birth kicked and killed the wheel-demon (Sakaṭāsura); his wonderful palms bearing the divine signs of the discus and conch; the sweet red lips of the child whom every milkmaid lifted and hugged affectionately to kiss and drink; the mouth that once swallowed the entire Universe but now looks innocently as a child of a humble milkmaid. Look at his bewitching eyes, eyebrows, forehead and the black curly hair—all so charming—one would not easily take away one's eyes looking at him."

[*Periyāḷvār Tirumoḻi*, I, 2]

Beckoning the Moon

In a decad known as *ambuli-parvam,* Periyāḷvār as Yasoda addresses the moon to come and play with her child Kṛṣṇa. A few verses are freely translated here:

Oh the Great Moon! My beloved child is waving His tiny hands and beckons you. If you wish to come and play with this child of black beauty, do not hide yourself behind the clouds but rush forth quickly and play happily.

Oh Moon! However much you make yourself resplendent by surrounding yourself with effulgence, you cannot stand comparison with the face of my child (the Lord of Venkatam). Swiftly you come before His waving hands start aching.

Oh the Great Moon! Don't ignore Him as a mere child. Know you well that He is the one who once (swallowed the Universe and) reclined on the banyan leaf. If He gets angry, He would spring forth and catch you. So come running and play with Him joyfully.

[*Ibid.*, I, 4]

Excerpts from Āṇḍāḷ's Tiruppāvai

The month of Margali (Mrigasirsha) has arrived and this auspicious full moon day, dear maidens of prosperous Ayarpadi (Gokulam), with pretty jewels, all of you who desire to bathe come along. He who is the son of Nandagopal, possessing a sharp spear and stern in his punishment, He who is the lion-cub of Yasoda, of beautiful eyes, with His dark cloud-like body, lotus red eyes and effulgent face like the rays of the Sun and the Moon. He is Narayana. He will give us—He alone will give us and only to us the drum required for the vow we have undertaken, the fulfilment of which will bring us the praise of the world.

[v. 1]

xxxx xxxx

Trailing the cows we go to the woods and eat our food there. Your birth in the unintelligent shepherd class of ours is our good fortune. Oh Govinda, perfect one, our kinship with you can never be snapped either by you or by us. If we, ignorant girls, out of our abundant love have addressed you by small (inferior) names, Oh Lord, you do not get angry, but do grant us the drum.

[v. 28]

In the small hours of the dawn, we come to worship you and glorify your golden lotus feet. Oh Govinda! be pleased to note the real purpose of this. Born in the shepherd class which lives by grazing the cows, you should not decline the services offered by us. We have not come to receive the *Parai* (drum) from you. We are one with you for seven times seven births and we shall serve you alone. Convert all our (other) desires (into a desire for you).

[v. 29]

Āṇḍāḷ's Nācciār Tirumoḻi

Nācciār Tirumoḻi is a love-song par excellence that proclaims the poignant emotions of a lovelorn soul. In the mysticism of Vaiṣṇava Saints, the game of love consists of *visleṣa* and *samslēṣa*, the experience of separation and union respectively. Āṇḍāḷ's hymns, like those of Meera of later times, exemplify this experience.

Oh Cuckoo! my body cannot endure the pain of separation; it thins out so much that my bangles slip out; wounded by His love, my mind dies slowly;

yet I do not see Him anywhere approach me. I am tossed in the sea of misery since I am bereft of my Lord, my only boat. My eyes have forgotten to sleep; the spring of my mouth and bosom dry out. Even cool wind and tender moon torture me. If you do not call Narayana today I will give up my life.

[*NT*, 5; verses 4 to 10]

The following excerpts are from Mahakavi Subrahmanya Bharati's translation of some verses of Āṇḍāḷ's *Nācciār Tirumoḻi*:

Ye others cannot conceive of His love that I bear for Kṛṣṇa And your warnings to me are in vain like the pleadings of the mute with the deaf. The boy who left His mother's home and was reared by a different mother—Oh take me forth to His city of Mathura where He won the field without fighting the battle and leave me there.

xxxx xxxx

Oh grieve not, ye mothers. None can know of this strange malady of mind. Of the colour of the blue sea is a certain youth—the gentle caress of His hands will heal me, surely.

On the bank of the waters He ascended the Kadamba tree and He leaped to His dance, the dance of war, on the hood of the snake. Oh take me forth to the bank of that lake and leave me there.

[*NT*, 12; v. 1 and 5]

From Āṇḍāḷ's Dream Wedding

As the drums beat and the conches blow long under the canopy of pearls; my endearing Lord Madhusudan came and grasped me by the hand.

So I dreamt, my dear friend!

[v. 6.6]

Now and for successive generations our protector Narayana held my toe by His auspicious hands and placed it on the stone-mortar.

So I dreamt, my dear friend!

[v. 6.8]

Nammāḻvār's Hymns

The story of your birth and growth here (in this world) and your causing the Great Bhārata War, the help you rendered to the Pāṇḍavas and several such wondrous acts have cast a spell to bind me to you, the splendid light of Heaven! You are in my heart melting it and consuming my very spirit.

When shall I join you?

[*TM*, 5; 10, 1]

xxxx xxxx

Rice that is eaten
Water that is drunk and betel that is chewed
And everything else
Are my Lord Kaṇṇan (Kṛṣṇa)
So she cries, the young gazelle
And eyes brimming with tears
She goes seeking
Asking where on this earth
He and His fame, dwell rich,
And the place she selects
And enters Tirukkōilūr.

(These are the wailing words of the mother of the lovelorn girl.)

[*Tiruvāymoḷi*, 6; 7, 1]

—Translation by A. Srinivasa Raghavan in *Nammāḷvār*
[Sahitya Academy, New Delhi, 1982, p. 43]

Subrahmanya Bharati on Kṛṣṇa

The great nationalist poet Mahakavi Subrahmanya Bharati (1882-1921) was profoundly inspired by many facets of Kṛṣṇa and expressed his awe and admiration for Him in several of his beautiful poems which have become extremely popular in Tamilnadu. Describing Kṛṣṇa 'my beloved', 'my inseparable companion', 'my mother', 'my teacher', 'my God'—he composed poems on each one of them. Some of them he himself translated into English verse. Here are a few samples from his famous poem entitled *In each other's arms*:

(The Supreme Deity styled here as Kṛṣṇa is imaged as the beloved woman and the human soul as the lover)

Thou to me, the flowing Light
And I to thee, discerning sight;
Honied blossom thou to me
Bee enchanted I to thee;
O Heavenly Love, O nectar-spray
with faltering tongue and words that pant
Thy glories, here, I strive to chant
Rain that singeth, thou to me
Peacock dancing, I to thee
Thou to me the juice of grape

xxxx xxxx

Silver Moolight thou to me
Exulting Ocean I to thee
Thou, the basic harmony
I, the song that moveth free;
Dear as eyesight, Krishna mine

xxxx xxxx

As Life to Pulse and Gold to rings,
As star to planet, Soul to things,
So Krishna, Love, art thou to me,
Thou, the Force, I, Victory—
And all the joys of Heavens and Earth
In thee, O Krishna, have their birth
Eternal Glory, endless Might
O Heart of Mine, O Light, O Light!

[C. Subrahmanya Bharati,
Agni and Other Poems etc., op. cit.]

BIBLIOGRAPHY

Epigraphy

Annual Reports on South Indian Epigraphy.

A Topographical List of the Inscriptions of the Madras Presidency, 3 Vols., (Ed.) V. Rangacharya, Madras, 1917.

Epigraphia Indica (E.I.).

Kanyākumāri Kalveṭṭukal, 5 Vols., Dept. of Archaeology, Govt. of Tamilnadu, Madras, 1972.

South Indian Inscriptions.

South Indian Temple Inscriptions, Ed. by Subramanian, T.N., Madras.

Ten Pandyan Copper Plates, Tamil Varalatru Kazhagam, Madras, 1967.

Thirty Pallava Copper Plates, Tamil Varalatru Kazhagam, Madras, 1966.

Topographical List of Inscriptions in Tamilnadu and Kerala, T.V. Mahalingam, I.C.H.R., New Delhi.

Literature

Āchāryahṛdayam, Alagiya Manavala Perumal Nayanar with translation, Naidu, Puroshottam, Madras, 1965.

Āgama Prāmanya, Ed. Misra Sastri.

Ainkurunūru, Auvai S. Duraisami Pillai (Ed.).

Ashtadhyāyi, Panini (Tr.) Vasu, S.L., Allahabad, 1891-98.

Ashta Prabandham, Pillai Perumal Iyangar, Madras, 1904.

Bhāgavata Purāṇa, Veda Vyas, Ed. Sastri, J.L., Eg. tr. Delhi, 1978.

Bhāgavatam (Tamil), Chevvai Sūduvar, Tirupati, 1949.

Bhārata Venbā, Perundevunar, Ed. by Aiyar, A.G., 1925.

Bhārata Venbā, Perundevunar, Ed. Muthuratna Mudaliyar, Tanjore, 1950.

Dēsikar Prabandham, Vedānta Desika, Ed. & Com. by Srirama Desikacharya, Tanjore, 1944.

Gōdāstuti, Vedānta Desika, Desika Stotramala, Tanjore, 1966.

Gōpālavimsati, Vedānta Desika, Desika Stotramala, Tanjore, 1966.

Guruparampara Prabhavam, Pinbalagiya Perumal Jeer.

Harivamsa, Translated by Dutt, M.N., Calcutta, 1897.

Harivamsa, Ed. by Vaidya, P.L., Pune, 1969.

Kalingattu Parani, Jayankondar, Ed. Puliyur Kesikan, Madras, 1940.

Kalitthokai, Ed. Puliyurkesikan, Madras, 1940.

Koyiloḷugu, Ed. Krishnaswami Iyangar, Tiruchi, 1976.

Kṛṣṇakarṇāmrita, Lilasukha, Ed. De, S.K., Dacca, 1938.

Maduraikānchi, Ed. U.V. Swaminatha Iyer, 1956.

Manimekalai, Ed. by S.K. Aiyengar.

Muppattārāyirappaḍi (*Īḍu*), Vadakku Tiruvidi Pillai, Ed. S. Krishnamachary, Madras, 1925, 1930 (Commentary on Nammalvar's *Tiruvaymoli*).

Nālāyira Divya Prabandham (with commentary) Annangaracharya, P.B. Kanchipuram, 1956.

Nālāyira Divya Prabandham, Ed. Krishnaswamy Iyangar, Tiruchi, 1981.

Naṟṟinai, Ed. Puliyur Kesikan, Madras.

Paripāḍal, Ed. Puliyur Kesikan, Madras.

Pattupāttu, Tr. by J.V. Chelliah, Madras, 1962.

Puranānūru, Ed. & Com. Puliyur Kesikan, Madras, 1977.

Rāmānuja Nūtrantati, Nitayanusantanam.

Ṛg Vēda, R.T.H. Griffith (Tr.), Benaras, 1897.

Satapata Brāhmaṇa, J. Eggling (Tr.), Oxford, 1882-1900.

Silappadikāram, Dikshitar, V.R.R. (Ed.) 1939; also Tr. by Alain Danielou, New York, 1965.

Silparatna, Tr. by Navalpakkam Devanathachari, Tanjore, 1961.

Srimad Bhagavat Gītā, Com. by Anna, Madras, 1945.

Srimad Bhagavat Gītā, S. Satyamurti Ayyangar, Madras, 1945.

Srimad Bhāgavata Purāṇa, Goswami, C.L., Gorakhpur, 1971.

Sri Vachana Bhūshana Sāram, Annangarachariar, P.B., Kanchipuram, 1927.

Tiruppāvai, Andal Com. Periyavacchan Pillai, Madras, Ed. S. Krishnamacharya.

Tiruvāymoḻi, Nammalvar, Ed. & Com. Annangarachariar, 2 Vols., Kanchipuram, 1951.

Tiruvāymoḻi, Ittin Tamilakkam, Purushottam Naidu, B.R., Madras.

Tolkāppiyam, Tolkappiyar Com. Nachinarkiniyar.

Viṣṇu Purāṇa (Tr.) H.W. Wilson, Ed. F. Hall, London, 1870.

Villi Bhāratam, Villiputturar, Comm. V.M. Gopala Krishnamacharya, Madras.

Yādavabhyudayam, Vedānta Desika.

Published Works

Aiyangar, M.S., *Tamil Studies*, Madras, 1914.

Aiyangar, P.T.S., *History of the Tamils*, Madras, 1929.

Aiyangar, S.K., *Religion of the Tamils of Sangam Age*, Calcutta, 1923.

———, *Some Contribution of South India to Indian Culture*, Calcutta, 1923.

———, *Early History of Vaiṣṇavism in South India*, Madras, 1920.

Aiyar, P.V. Jagadisa, *South Indian Shrines*, Madras, 1920.

Ansari, Z.A. and Mali, M.S., *Excavations at Dwaraka*, Poona, 1966.

Archer, W.G., *The Loves of Kṛṣṇa*, New York, 1957.

Arunachalam, M., *Tamil Ilakkiya Varalāru*, 5 Vols.

Ayyar, E.S. Varadaraja, *History of Tamil Literature.*

Balasubramaniyan, S.R., *Four Chola Temples*, Bombay, 1963.

———, *Early Chola Art*, Bombay, 1966.

———, *Middle Chola Temples*, 1975.

———, *Later Chola Temples*, 1980.

Banerjea, J.N., *Development of Hindu Iconography*, Calcutta, 1956.

Banerjee, P., *Early Indian Religions*, Delhi, 1973.

———, *Life of Kṛṣṇa in Indian Art*, Delhi, 1978.

Barnett, L.D., *Hindu Gods and Heroes*, London, 1923.

Barrett, Douglas, *Early Chola Bronzes.*

Basham, A.L., *The Wonder that was India*, London, 1956.

Benjamin, Preciado-Solis, *The Kṛṣṇa Cycle in the Purāṇas*, Delhi, 1984.

Bhandarkar, R.G., *Vaiṣṇavism, Saivism and Minor Religious Systems*, Poona, 1938.

Bhattacharya, Haridass, *The Cultural Heritage of India*, Vol. IV, Calcutta, 1958.

Bhattacharya, S.K., *Kṛṣṇa Cult.*

Brow, W.N., *Mythology of the Ancient World*, New York, 1961.

Champakalakshmi, R., *Vaiṣṇava Iconography in the Tamil Country*, Orient Longman, 1981.

Chattopadhyaya, B.C., *Kṛṣṇa-charita*, Calcutta.

Das, Bhagwan, *Krishna*, Adyar, 1929.

Desai, Kalpana S., *Iconography of Viṣṇu in North India*, New Delhi, 1973.

Deshmukh, P.S., *The Origin and Development of Religion in Vedic Literature*, London, 1933.

Dikshitar, V.R.R., *Studies in Tamil Literature and History,* London, 1923.

Dowson, John, *A Classical Dictionary of Hindu Mythology and Religions, etc.*, London, 1953.

Elmore, W.T., *Dravidian Gods in Modern Hinduism,* Oxford, 1920.

Farquhar, J.N., *An Outline of the Religious Literature of India.*

Francois Cros and R. Nagaswamy, *Uttaramerur, Legends, History and Monuments,* Pondicherry, 1970.

Gangoly, O.C., *South Indian Bronzes,* Calcutta, 1915.

———, *The Art of the Pallavas,* Calcutta, 1957.

Gonda, J., *Aspects of Early Vishnuism,* Utrecht, 1954.

Grierson, G.A., *The Krishnavatara Lila,* Calcutta, 1928.

Gupte, R.S., *Iconography of the Hindus,* Bombay, 1972.

———, *Buddhists and Jains.*

Hari Rao, V.N., *Srirangam Temple,* 1967.

Hardy, Friedhelm, *Viraha-Bhakti, The Early History of Kṛṣṇa Devotion,* Oxford, 1983.

Hopkins, E.W., *The Religions of India,* Boston, 1895.

Hooper, J.M.S., *Hymns of Alvars,* Heritage of India Series, 1929.

Hudson, Dennis, *Srimad Bhagavata Purana in Stone, Journal of Vaisnava Studies,* Vol. 3, No. 3 (1925). Also Vol. 2, No. 2.

Iyangar, M. Raghava, *Vēlir Varalāru.*

———, *Ālvārgal-Kālanilai,* 1929.

———, *Āraycchi-thoguti,* 1938.

Jagadeesan, N., *History of Vaishnavism in Tamil Country,* Madurai, 1977.

Jagannathachariar, C., *Tiruppāvai—Textual, Literary and Critical Study.*

Jaiswal, S., *The Origin and Development of Vaishnavism,* New Delhi, 1967.

Joshi, N.P., *Mathura Sculptures,* Mathura, 1966.

———, *Iconography of Balarāma,* New Delhi.

Jouveau-Dubreuil, G., Tr. by Martin, A.C., *Iconography of South India,* Paris, 1937.

Kanakasabai, *The Tamils 1800 Years Ago,* Madras, 1956.

Kailasapathy, K., *Tamil Heroic Poetry,* Oxford, 1968.

Karashima, Noboro, *A Concordance of Names in Chola Inscriptions,* Madurai, 1978.

Keith, A.B., *The Religion and Philosophy of the Vedas and Upanishads,* Cambridge, 1925.

Kinsley, R. David, *The Sword and the Flute,* Vikas Publications, 1975.

———, *The Divine Player* (A study of Kṛṣṇa Lila), Delhi.

Krishna, Nandita, *The Art and Iconography of Viṣṇu-Nārāyaṇa,* Bombay, 1980.

Kumarappa, R., *The Hindu Conception of the Deity*, London, 1934.

Leach, Maria, *Standard Dictionary of Folklore, Mythology and Legend*, New York.

MacCrindle, *Ancient India as described by Megasthenes and Arrian.*

Marr, J. Ralston, *The Eight Anthologies*, Madras, 1985.

Mazumdar, A.K., *Bhakti Renaissance*, Bombay, 1965.

Mazumdar, B.B., *Kṛṣṇa in Legend and History*, Calcutta, 1969.

Mazumdar, R.C. (Ed.), *The Classical Age*, Bombay, 1954.

———, *The Age of Imperial Unity*, Bombay, 1953.

Mehta, R.D., *Early Indian Religious Thought*, London, 1956.

Morgan, K.W. (Ed.), *The Religion of the Hindus*, New York, 1953.

Mukerjee, Radha Kamal, *The Lord of the Autumn Moods*, Bombay, 1957.

Natarajan, B., *Sri Kṛṣṇa Leela Tarangini by Narayana Tirtha*, Madras, 1988.

Pal, D.N., *Kṛṣṇa—His Life and Teachings*, Calcutta, 1901.

Pandey, R.K., *Concept of Avatāras.*

Pillai, K.K., *Social Life of the Tamils*, Madras, 1975.

———, *The Sucindram Temple*, Madras, 1953.

Raghavan, V., *The Indian Heritage*, Bangalore, 1953.

Ramachandran, T.N., *Tirupparuttikunram and its Temples*, Madras, 1934.

Ramachandran T.N. and Gravely, F.H., *Hindu Metal Images in the Madras Museum*, 1932.

Raman, K.V., *Pāndiyar Varalāru*, Madras, 1977.

———, *Sri Varadarajaswami Temple, Kanchi*, New Delhi, 1972.

———, *The Early History of Madras Region*, 1959.

Rao, M. Rama, *Temples of Tirumalai and Tirupati.*

Rao, T.A.G., *Elements of Hindu Iconography*, 2 Vols., Varanasi, 2nd Ed. 1971.

Raychaudhuri, H., *Early History of Vaishnava Sect*, Calcutta, 1936.

Reddiar Subbu, N., *Religion and Philosophy of Nālāyiram*, Tirupati, 1977.

Sahai, Bhagwant, *Iconography of Minor Hindu and Buddhist Deities*, Delhi, 1975.

Sanjivi, N., *Sanga Ilakkiya Āraycchi Attavanai.*

Sanyal, Nisikanta, *Kṛṣṇa Chaitanya*, Madras, 1933.

Sastri, K.A.N., *Development of Religion in South India*, Madras, 1963.

———, *History of South India*, Madras, 1955.

———, *The Cōḷas*, Madras, 1935.

Sastri, R.V. Panduranga and V. Athariale, *Life of Lord Kṛṣṇa*, Bombay, 1975.

Schulberg, Lucille, *Historic India*, Netherlands, 1969.

Sharma, B.N., *Festivals of India*, Delhi, 1978.

Shulman, D. David, *The King and the Clown in South Indian Myth and Poetry*, Princeton.

———, *Tamil Temple Myths*, Princeton, 1980.

Singer, Milton (Ed.), *Kṛṣṇa: Myths, Rites and Attitudes*, Chicago, 1966.

Sircar, D.C., *Studies in the Religious Life of Ancient and Medieval India*, Delhi.

Sivaramamurti, C., *Indian Sculpture*, Delhi, 1961.

———, *South Indian Paintings*, New Delhi, 1968.

———, *South Indian Bronzes*, New Delhi, 1963.

Spink, W.M., *Kṛṣṇa Mandala*, Ann Arbor, 1971.

Srinivasan, K.R., *The Dharmaraja Ratha & its Sculptures*, New Delhi, 1975.

———, *Cave Temples of the Pallavas*, New Delhi.

Srinivasan, P.R., *Bronzes of South India*, Madras, 1963.

Tirumalai, R., *Rajendra Vinnagar*, Madras, 1982.

Varadachari, V., *Āgamas and South Indian Vaishnavism*, Madras, 1982.

Venkatacharya, K.K.A., *Āgamas and Silpa*, Bombay, 1984.

Vidyanandan, S., *Tamilar Salbu*, Madras, 1971.

Viji, Chitra, *Srirangam Paintings*, Ph.D. thesis of Madras University (Unpublished).

Vivekananda Patrika (Kendra Ed.), *Temple India*, Madras, 1981.

Vivekananda Patrika (Kendra Ed.), *Indian Paintings through the Ages*, Madras, 1982.

Whitehead, Rev. Father, *The Village Gods of South India*, Oxford, 1921.

Zevelebil, K.V., *The Smile of Murugan*, 1973.

———, *Tamil Literature*, (Ed.) J. Gonda, 1973.

Zimmer, H., *Myths and Symbols in Indian Art and Civilisation*, New York, 1962.

Journals

Artibus Asiae

Gītāchārya, Madras (Tamil)

Indian Antiquary

Journal of Indian History

Journal of the Institute of Traditional Cultures, University of Madras, Madras

Journal of Oriental Research, Madras

Journal of Royal Asiatic Society, Bombay

Journal of Vaiṣṇava Studies, Washington, D.C.

Lalit Kalā

Madras University Historical Series

Quarterly Journal of the Mythic Society, Bangalore

Rāmānujan (Tamil), Kanchi

Rāmānuja-Vāni (Tamil), Madras

Sudarsanam (Tamil), Tiruchirapalli

Transactions of Archaeological Society of South India, Madras

Travancore Archaeological Series

INDEX